CITY LIGHTS
REVIEW

Number One

Edited by
Lawrence Ferlinghetti and Nancy J. Peters

CITY LIGHTS BOOKS
San Francisco

STAFF EDITORS:

Robert Sharrard
Amy Scholder
Stephen Ronan

Designed by Patricia Fujii
Typesetting by Re/Search
Cover illustration by Topor

"The Global Drift toward Nuclear War" by Noam Chomsky is from a speech broadcast by KPFA/FM Pacifica radio in Berkeley, California.

Illustrations by Roland Topor by permission of the artist.

"Keeping True to the Earth" by Edward Abbey was first published in *Earth First!*

"Then" by Marilyn Hacker first appeared in *Yellow Silk Journal.*

Library of Congress Cataloging-in-Publication Data
Main entry under title:

City lights review.

I. Ferlinghetti, Lawrence. II. Peters, Nancy J.
(Nancy Joyce) III. City lights (San Francisco, Calif.)

AC5.C57 1987   081   86-33421
ISBN 0-87286-200-3 (pbk.)

City Lights Books are printed on acid-free paper.

CITY LIGHTS BOOKS are edited by Lawrence Ferlinghetti & Nancy J. Peters and published at the City Lights Bookstore, 261 Columbus Avenue, San Francisco, CA 94133

CITY LIGHTS REVIEW NUMBER 1

Just as City Lights Bookstore is a literary meeting place, this *Review* aims to furnish a similar kind of locale in print, an "open space" for people who have a mind to speak.

Our concerns are with live poetry, engaged literature, radical politics, and deep ecology. These ideas are very much in the tradition of former City Lights journals and anthologies published in the past quarter-century. The last *Journal for the Protection of All Beings* co-published in 1978 with *Co-Evolution Quarterly* was centered on "how to liberate mind & body and protect endangered species (including ourselves) from pathogenic industrial civilization." And we ran a poem by Bertolt Brecht which ends:

> What times are these
> when a conversation about trees
> is almost a crime
> because it includes
> so much silence
> about so many outrages!

How the meaning of that poem has changed today when, given the increasing death of life being engendered by our ecologically-insane industrial perplex, it is almost a crime *not* to talk of trees.

The last thirteen years of this century give us a great opportunity to prove that Man is not too stupid and too greedy to save himself and all life from extinction. There may be a real opening in that eternal chess match between Eros and Death, between the free individual and materialist militarist mass society. We see this opening in a growing awareness that situates Man—in the perspective of deep ecology—as one breathing part of a universe which is itself one living organism affected by everything we do, as the quivering of a star makes earth shiver.

This sense of the linkage of all things leads naturally to a maximalist rather than a minimalist view of life and art in which the artist and poet are the divining rods or antennae on the frontiers of new consciousness.

We are looking for the diviners.

TABLE OF CONTENTS

WHO'S WHO IN THE REVIEW

EDWARD ABBEY, *Earth First!* hero, is the valiant author of *The Monkey Wrench Gang* and *Desert Solitaire.*

IVAN ARGÜELLES is a poet and librarian at the University of California, Berkeley.

JULIAN BECK co-founded the Living Theatre with Judith Malina.

ERIC BENTLEY, the drama critic and translator, recently published *The Brecht Memoir* and the *Pirandello Commentaries.*

JULIEN BLAINE, born in the Mouth of the Rhone in 1942, is the author of a dozen books, the founder of numerous transcultural revues, and director of the annual International Festival of Poetry at Cogolin (France). Our selection is drawn from his *13427 Poèmes Metaphysiques* (Editeurs Evidant).

IAIN BOAL is a Celt whose special interest is linguistics and the critical history of technology. He teaches a Plato-to-Nato course at Stanford University.

JAMES BROOK is an editor and poet whose translation of Alberto Savinio's *Lives of the Gods* is about to be published by Performing Arts.

ERNESTO CARDENAL is an "exteriorista" poet, priest, and Nicaragua's Minister of Culture; *To Nicaragua, with Love* is his most recent collection of poetry, published by City Lights Books.

NOAM CHOMSKY is the pre-eminent philosopher, writer, and linguistics professor at M.I.T.

TOM CLARK's ferocious new novel *The Exile of Celine* is just out.

ANDREI CODRESCU, editor of *Exquisite Corpse,* can be heard on National Public Radio's "All Things Considered;" his commentaries are collected in *A Craving for Swan.*

ADAM CORNFORD is Director of the Poetics Program at New College of California; his new book of poetry *Animations* will be published by City Lights.

PHILIP DAUGHTRY first saw the light in a coal-mining village outside Newcastle, England; he has published three books of poems.

ALYSSA ERDLEY is an architect in Oakland, California who is now preparing a collection of her metaromantic stories for publication.

LYDIA DAVIS, known for her masterful translations of Maurice Blanchot and others, last year published a third volume of her own striking short prose, *Break It Down.*

LAWRENCE FERLINGHETTI denies any knowledge of the individual fitting his description wearing a bandana disguise and posting banners reading "Hayduke Lives" in the vicinity of Columbus and Broadway, San Francisco.

JEAN FERRY, born in 1906 in France, was an expert on Raymond Roussel and wrote oneiric explorations such as "She Woke Me Up So I Killed Her."

BRIGITTE FONTAINE is a French feminist fabulist.

CHARLES HENRI FORD perambulates the literary and art worlds of Kathmandu, Crete, and New York City.

FEDERICO GARCIA LORCA, the Andalusian poet and dramatist, was assassinated by Falangists early in the Spanish civil war. His *Poem of the Deep Song* is forthcoming from City Lights Books.

ALLEN GINSBERG's latest books are *The Annotated Howl* and the very strange *White Shroud*.

ROBERT GLÜCK is the author of *Elements of a Coffee Service* (1982) and *Jack the Modernist* (1986).

SUSAN GRIFFIN, feminist theorist and poet, is completing *The First and the Last: a Woman Looks at War*, which examines the relationships between social and sexual secrecy and militarism.

MARILYN HACKER, recipient of the National Poetry Award, has just published her fourth book of poetry, *Love, Death, and the Changing of the Seasons*.

JESSICA HAGEDORN, now writing *Dogeaters*, is enlivening the New York poetry scene as a performance artist and editor of *The Poetry Project Newsletter*.

DEBORA IYALL has recorded her first solo album "Strange Language," following three albums with the group Romeo Void.

PHILIP LAMANTIA, poet and passional ornithologist, is the creator of *Meadowlark West*.

JAMES LAUGHLIN is the author of *The Master of Those Who Know* and the founder of the New Directions Publishing Corp.

REINHARD LETTAU won a German radio award for his radical play *Breakfast Conversations in Miami*. He teaches in the literature department at University of California, San Diego, where he was a close friend of Herbert Marcuse.

HENRI MICHAUX, the French poet, painter, and essayist, died in Paris in 1984.

ABD AL-HAYY MOORE, originator of the Floating Lotus Opera, is the publisher of Zil Zal Press and a producer of the Santa Barbara Arts Festival.

ALEJANDRO MURGUIA fought in the final offensive of the Nicaraguan revolution at Peñas Blancas in 1979. He records his experiences in his novel-in-progress *Southern Front*.

ANTONIO MACHADO (1875-1939) was one of Spain's greatest 20th-century poets.

FAE MYENNE NG has published short fiction in literary journals and has taught in writing programs at University of California, Berkeley and Santa Cruz.

CESARE PAVESE (1908-1950) was an Italian writer of the first rank, an antifascist always on the side of the oppressed.

MARIE PONSOT's first book was published in City Lights' Pocket Poets Series; her most recent collection of poems is *Admit Impediment*.

ANTONIO PORTA was a founder of Italy's "Novissimi" poets whose style was bittersweet, defiant, and subversive; his *Kisses from Another Dream* is forthcoming from City Lights Books.

RODRIGO REY ROSA, one of Guatemala's most imaginative young writers, is the author of *The Beggar's Knife*.

JANET RICHARDS incisively described the New York and San Francisco avant-garde of the 1940s and 1950s in her memoir *Common Soldiers*.

ALBERTO SAVINIO (1891-1952) was the brother of Giorgio di Chirico; Apollinaire said of him, "as a poet, painter, playwright, and musician, he was like a genius of the Tuscan Renaissance."

ALFONSINA STORNI (1892-1938) was an Argentine poet who was at once radically democratic, feminist, and deeply romantic.

MUTSUO TAKAHASHI is one of Japan's brightest contemporary poets. His selected poems, *A Bunch of Keys*, was published in 1984.

NADJA TESICH was born in Yugoslavia and is a film maker, screenwriter, and playwright. "Mission" is from her novel *About that Time*.

ROLAND TOPOR is a "black humor" artist who influenced a whole generation. He recently designed marionettes for "Marquis Chien de Sade"; and played the role of Renfield in Werner Herzog's "Nosferatu."

NANOS VALAORITIS, translator, hermeneutist, and Delphic poet, teaches at San Francisco State University.

MARIE WILSON is a painter of mythical, emblematic images. She teaches in Berkeley and is preparing an exhibition of her new work.

MICHAEL WOLFE's most visible book is *Invisible Weapons*.

Roland Topor

from

The Disappearance of the Outside

Prologue: Notes from Underground

ANDREI CODRESCU

My friend Greg, a professional philosopher, just bought his first computer. Millions of words have been written about the changed relations between writer and writing because of the computer. In spite of it, every new user has to talk about it. It is a fin de siècle *rite de passage*, an initiation into contemporaneity. "I used to look out the window a lot when I wrote," Greg said. "Now I find myself looking at the words I have just finished writing."

"Very soon," I said, "you will not need the computer to see words on a screen. There will be words on a screen *everywhere* you look. They will be the words you just thought." I should have said, "the words you just thought you thought."

With the computer, the philosopher's window disappears. He will be staring henceforth at his own propositions. Interiority has taken command. Insofar as Greg is a *professional* philosopher, the computer only formalizes a *fait accompli*. It is only amateurs who feel keenly the loss of the sky.

What Greg had been seeing out his window had been rapidly diminishing in any case. Even the great forests of Brazil are under attack. It is possible that if Greg had been an amateur he could have seen these forests, and perhaps all that is left of the wilderness standing there before his window in mute supplication. His window would have given out into the places where the roads don't go. Even then, he would have only seen them through the glass, Mies glass no doubt, through the fetish of modern art which separates the eyes from all the other senses. It is not only the wilderness that dies outside Greg's window, it is also the sensual life of humans, our own inner outside.

The computer screen completes the last turn to the interior. "The word," William Burroughs said, "is a virus." The word, to be more specific, is the virus of interiority. The computerized word is interiority squared. The word

1

on TV = the word × the image. The way out of the mirror is cut off.

In the past ten years the outside has greatly diminished in all its dimensions: geography, imagination, liberty. Transcendence has closed shop. The unknown, once accessible in various ways, has been sealed off at the borders. The police have arrived everywhere: in the East it is uniformed police. In the West it is the invisible police of image manipulation. The militarization of the planet is complete. Outer space is being militarized. "There are no more civilians" (Paul Virilio). We have been drafted against our will like peasants in the Middle Ages, dragged off to war without even noticing it. Power goes unquestioned because our eyes are full of images that obscure it. The world outside the Western borders has been closed *ahead* of the expansion of markets: the psychic enclosure now issues us a completely new set of eyes. In the East, the paper *dokument* still does the job. Ah, Mayakovsky, how you waved your red passport!

The new interior of the computerized fin de siècle is not the interior of the earlier decades. It is an interior that has learned to mimic some of the characteristics of the outside. It has learned, above all, to project a sense of infinity. The human interiors until now had always been defined in relation to their fragility in the great cosmic outside. The womb, the cave, the house, even the armor, have been small markers of presence in a vast and wildly alive cosmos.

The new imperial interior has brought revolt to a standstill by projecting the innocent simplicity of its own control machinery. It is, of course, quite beautiful. It is also expandable in any given direction. The mechanisms by which we are made to do the things we do stand exposed before us. How could we harm these things of which we are a part? Things that we can *see*, including the part that we are? Even if the part we are is the part that gets trampled? How can we steal when stealing will increase prices all of us will then be forced to pay? How can we attack a particularly vile war machine when this war machine defends *us* against another vile war machine?

The notion of community was stripped of its difference. No longer does community (*any* community) stand outside the State, in direct challenge to it. All communities have been expanded through a neat trick of generalization to *become* the State. When community was a means of resistance, it was constituted to point *outward*. The artificial community designed by the state points inward: it is a producer of interior. The techniques by which the Western State has insinuated itself at the heart of community are visual.

As the interior becomes all there is, there is less and less to oppose to it. There is nothing to compare it to. The memory of the outside is also a form of interiority: the outside resides *in* memory. It can be argued that the interior is the space where everything disappears, including the bombardments of the media. Jean Baudrillard sees the mass as a black hole, capable of absorbing anything, reflecting everything, giving up nothing (*In the Shadow of the Silent Majorities*). If this is the case, the only thing that exists in the interior is a hyperconformism, a flattening out of all differences, a mechanical and collective mass that is either manipulated or manipulates the social, political, economical, and philosophical attempts on it. This kind of interior can only be the result of an institutional philosophy however, a projection of bureaucratic automatism that severs the organs of dissent, including most importantly the mouth. Hence the silent majority. This philosophy is historically recent, and it has to do less with ideology than with the technological structures that now link everyone in a new electronic nervous system. The new passivity is the result of hormonal-electrical engineering. We are being fed salt petre, on the one hand, and ginseng on the other. We are being castrated of expression but kept excited for consumption. That explains both the mind-boggling conformism of the mass and the extraordinary empty physical vitality that possesses it (jogging).

Roland Barthes and the French school expanded the words "writing" and "reading" to take in everything. The world is a text. Therefore it can be read. Previously "dense" areas become intelligible: signs connect in a language. The world becomes flat like the page. It is, of course, a text without "author." Authorial intention "writes out." What it "writes in," the final readable version is only a record by default of what it has suppressed. The human library is thus the repository of repression. Only the official (written) version survives. But the repressed returns, will return, when the author is removed. Then the erased text reappears, a little like restoring a suppressed poem from a typewriter's correction ribbon. Or restoring an erased file on a disc. Modernism took the author as far as the author could go while remaining an author. Even as far as disappearing from the work. The New York school painters insisted on "flatness": it was the central dogma of their art. The tricks of perspective and the suspension of disbelief went out the same philosopher's window, seconds before it closed.

Reading the word's text is an activity that allows mystery only one virtue, that of being explicated. The whole world becomes a Borgesian library. Sections of this library are author-ized, others (the vast majority) are authorless. The spiral staircases that connect one section to another are a complex nervous system whose intricacies an explorer (reader) can travel forever.

This vision is not, however, one of unredeemed interiority, because the signs that can be read aren't just *there*. They also can be *invented*. The imagination can change, erase or increase the text in any direction it pleases. It is the demiurgic force, par excellence. It is trans-authorial: it uses the brain that uses the hand. It is everywhere creation occurs, and creation occurs everywhere. Most importantly, it exists in opposition to what it creates. Its creations are its enemies. In order to overcome them, and prevent itself from being marginalized, weakened and extinguished, it must create even more. Imagination is increased by the necessity to overcome its productions. It can only go forward, like Einstein's light, because it has no choice. The virtual and the created are at war. It is natural then that existing (institutional) interiority must first attack the imagination. Imagination looks exclusively outside: it can only face that way. Trespassing the borders of creation is its only job. Transgression, its *modus operandi*.

The integrity of the imagination is suffering mega-assaults at the moment. The fake imagination of the entertainment industry is seeking to replace the organic, primary, connected imagination of human beings. An ideology of the imagination (ideology = somebody else's ideas) is replacing the spontaneous practice of it. The institutionalization of the imagination is one of the main concerns (if not *the* main concern) of both major political interiorities. In the East, the crude hand of the State enters the process directly. In the West, the State replaces the free play of the mind with programming. The two modes, brutality and narcolepsy, respectively, have different effects.

If the text has its Lucifer in imagination, memory also has an angel who knows the way out, namely excess. To remember unabashedly, monstrously, sensually, is to test the convenient versions of the past. Remembering like this quickly exhausts the officially alloted quotas of nostalgia. The connection between memory and the outside is not simply one of containment. Memory contains a launch trigger. It can be operated both slow and fast. The slow trigger is made of painstaking emotional reconstruction. The fast trigger is chemical: LSD. Proust's madeleine is both. There are only words to tell us where Proust *really* went, but the words point in the same direction as the madeleine: out. This out happens to be the past, but it's a past experienced *now*.

Poetry is words pointing out. No one, least of all the poet, knows where he or she is heading. Control is words pointing in. Within the language of the world-as-is, only poetry points out: the words are magnetically aligned to the true outside. Official grammar is the magnet of interiority. Drawn by it, all words point in: the signs have been turned to point in. The job of the poet is to straighten out the signs to make them point out. The poetics of memory can join the poetics of experience under special circumstances, using Proust's LSD 25 madeleine. But one can only go so far, either slowly or fast, if the outside is objectively gone. Hopefully, it has only been diminished, and made harder to find. It has been "disappeared" like an Argentine prisoner or a Gulag *zek*.

If imagination is the irrepressible enemy of the text-as-is (the status quo), so is an excess of remembering. In the dual undoing of imagination and time-travel, the world's text unravels: it becomes poetry. The unpredictable returns the world to its state of mysterious wilderness. "Our job," said Lucian Blaga, "when confronted by a mystery, is not to explain it, but to enlarge it, to make it more mysterious." Out of the classroom, and into the unknown!

Of course, there is no reading without Marxism in contemporary criticism. The reason is that Marxism has abolished the unknown (or that capitalism has, in the Marxist view). They would have us believe that Rimbaud went as far as he did because that was the last escape into the last unknown possible while still maintaining authorship. It was the end of the individual, the end of the linearity of print. The expansion of markets in the 19th century all but eliminated the unknown. With Rimbaud went poetry and imagination because poetry and imagination can only go as far as the person travelling with them. Rimbaud, however, *abolished himself* before he could be so easily "read." He envisioned the coming of the "red cities," the advent of the collective Rimbaud, the mass acting like an intoxicated individual. And he wanted none of it. It is not capitalism that abolished the unknown of the individual but Rimbaud the individual who abolished capitalism, and all economic theory with it, including Marxism. The Marxists can rail on about "markets," they know nothing of the imagination. Imagination is demiurgic. It creates the markets it saturates, overthrows and transforms. The Marxists have no gods, therefore they cannot imagine it. They are without ontological memory: they do not remember either their conception or their origin. They have no world prior to ideology. They reproduce within the text of their own interpretations. Lately, they have even exchanged history for a reading of it. This is why the only Marxists to be found today are in universities. The determinism of the classroom is the only place where they can operate. The worker, that ideal history-making Marxist, has been eliminated by Marxist criticism. The worker has become a sign, a kind of prefix attached to certain borders.

In the Soviet Union the State is the sole reader of reality, and thus the only Marxist. The Marxist thinkers themselves have become parts of the speech of the State, bordering prefixes. The rigorous grammar of the State has only one enemy: writers.

The outside is a substance increased and diminished. The outside exists most importantly, and before anything, as *an appetite*. We are losing our appetites for everything: food, adventure, freedom. They are replaced by controlled cravings induced by visual and aural stimulation. At the same time we can see the diminishing of what lies outside ourselves, outside the feeble light of our cravings and their consumption needs. Fifty percent of the world's population will live in cities by year 2000, reads one headline. The other fifty percent will not have more room, however. They will be inhabiting prescribed areas on the edges of toxic pits. The environment will be rigorously gridded to serve the needs of the electronic brain. Every human being living now can see the shrinking of the world, and feel the effects of relentless metering. We don't even need facts and figures to see.

How do we see? In the same way that we *see* that no one is home before we even turn the key in the door, or sense the presence of an animal somewhere behind us without even turning. The animal is a machine and it hides no longer in the dark but it is always with us. Rationalists may try to convince us that the outside does not exist, but to deny the experience of it would be like denying childhood. The outside is not simply what is uncovered by our needs in search for satisfaction, the way people sometimes think of "growing up" as an enlargement of the area of experience. Neither the outside nor childhood are annexed zones of consciousness. They are not, either one of them, an unconscious. The outside exists both in a physical, geographical dimension, as parts of our planet yanked out of their specific ecology and made to turn about the petty tyranny of our desires, and in a metaphysical dimension, as an area accessible by religious feeling. In its physical sense it is the place where the human creature is equal to other living things, where it does not measure anything against itself, where indeed it can forget itself. In its metaphysical sense it is that place of dreaming, accessible by imagination and poetry, where we

have stubbornly insisted in going since we began as a species. That the two embodiments of the outside are disappearing together is the greatest tragedy that has befallen us so far, a tragedy much greater than an adverse history. Deprived of our ability to identify with nature and of the mythical imagination, we become no more than the slaves of machines, machines ourselves, slaves of slaves. The cybernetic view (man the splendid machine) finds no essential quarrel between biology and mechanics. Its key demand is efficiency. The communality of the species is enhanced by its functioning *more* not less like a machine. Marshall McLuhan says that Gutenberg invented the individual, but now the individual (the author) is finished. "Literacy stresses *lineality*, a one-thing-at-a-time awareness and mode of procedure. From it derive the assembly line and the order of battle, the managerial hierarchy and the departmentalization of scholarly decorum. Gutenberg gave us analysis and explosion. By fragmenting the field of perception and breaking information into static bits, we have accomplished wonders" (*The Agenbite of Outwit*). The electronic media, however, operates differently. It is simultaneous, auditory, global, tribal. It connects us all to the only job left: moving information. Work disappears. It will be done by the machines. But which machines? The *lesser* machines. The superior machines (us) will work at becoming more of a *single* organism. The individual dies for the species. The original program. Finis.

McLuhan's vision makes no room,

just as the State or the electronic nervous system makes no room, for the unpredictable, the asystemic, the imaginary. It is a closed and closing circuit. It cannot foresee its overthrow, and it knows nothing of the operation of mystery in the world. It is not demiurgic, it is cooperative. It conforms to its own ineluctability. The State and rationalism (religion before that) have always attempted and never succeeded in passing themselves off as irrevocable, necessary and ineluctable. It is the task of technology as the newest member of this triumvirate to finish the job.

Those who dismiss the anti-technological revolt as mere romantic nostalgia are not realists. They are agents of the machines. The job of the human organism is to survive. It will fend off any perceived threats to its integrity. The dread and horror we have been feeling since the advent of the industrial revolution is real. We have been seduced by machines, it is true, but the last two hundred years have not brought about an improvement of the species as a whole, nor have they created a better, stronger, freer individual. The connections between human bodies and the planet are being mediated by machines. We are becoming more like machines while machines are becoming more "human." Mass conformism brought to its present day apogee in the silent (surveyed) mass, has abandoned the planet. We live in Baudrillardian "hyper-reality," a mirage of mass media messages and simulation. The planet (the outside) is not within reach: we sense it, like a memory, as it is being murdered.

The outside is sometimes increased in unexpected ways. An excess of interiority can produce a wilderness. The great European city is an interiority gone over to wilderness, an overgrown inside. The point at which the city loses sight of the central plan and becomes an organic entity, it becomes "nature." Its doors are trees. The same phenomenon can occur within a social class, as it did in the 1960s when the well-regulated middle class produced an aberrant generation of children who became voluntary "outsiders." Cancer, our contemporary psycho-environmental disease par excellence, is also a wilderness grown within to spite the ways in which we have abandoned the earth. The interior of body and society depends on stability, on reasonable rules. When these are overcome, the wilderness returns, like the jungle through the asphalt in Miami.

Two decades ago "the doors of perception" were blown wide open and flying became commonplace. There was seemingly unlimited space. Drunk on so much outside, we took it for granted that our institutional life would soon be flooded by the infinite. We looked forward to *transparency*, to policy based on the awareness of light. Perhaps what we were experiencing was not the true outside (it could hardly be, in view of all the determinisms surrounding us) but only a glimpse of it through a briefly opened philosopher's window. What the glimpse revealed was the outside at possibly the same moment that it was disappearing. What lent substance to the glimpse was the ongoing war in Southeast Asia. From the brief meeting of the transcendent with the historical, there formed a certain critical authority, a certain weight. It was the palpable weight of this new resistance that almost amounted to a jailbreak. The personal, familial and societal structures all felt its impact. The institutions began to close in, to defend the marked (marketed) territories. The approaches to the outside were rapidly repressed, bought out, colonized, internalized, closed. The doors of perception were locked back up. The Oedipal doors were closed by worried parents with the hasty sacrifice of our generation. In tactical retreat, they wrote us off in order to save the younger siblings. A variety of techniques, from greater permissiveness to an increase of technical fantasies were employed. The next to the last slice of the American economic pie rotated suddenly into view on the lunch counter. Everyone scrambled for it, trying to finish school, to fit into a suit, to get a job. The social doors in front of the Oedipal doors were shut by the police with new paranoid fantasies about morality and race. The geographical doors were shut by closing any but the approved tourist tracks. The twin policemen of science and religion were posted at the doors of mystery. Gates to all experimental endeavor came clanging down all over the place.

The militarization of inner space was a two-decade project. The same agent was, in some cases, responsible for both liberation and re-entry. LSD 25, first introduced to civilians by the CIA, provided a brand new psychic field for the drama of our central metaphor. The inside and the outside, in the Taoist sense, are often interchangeable. They can, in fact, change places so fast, the being in transit is caught napping. Two decades ago, many young people, having gone to sleep inside, awakened under the stars. Today, the rare person going to sleep outside, is likely to awaken in prison. Even skid row parks, those few tolerated areas where the destitute can sleep, are being increasingly closed. In the Soviet Union and Eastern Europe there is no question of sleeping outside. The police arrest even those merely overcome by drowsiness. Even in what remains of the wilderness, sleep is only allowed in designated areas. The reconstructed universal prison of the 1980s is superior to the one we escaped from in the 1960s. The controllers know what to look for. But improved or not, the control valves that prevent the universe from flowing through us are still the same valves we had once breached. The brain, which is the valve room, was once bathed in the light of the outside. No amount of repair can straighten out the poetic damage to the bio-Oedipal-social cage. The State solution is the destruction of the outside itself, and of the only vehicles capable of reaching it: imagination and memory. Its job is the erasure of possibility, the absolute occupation of the unknown by what is known, the obliteration of mystery. The interiority of body, family and State is waging *jihad* against the eternally generative universe.

The invasion of the outside in the 1960s transcended politics. The approaches of the two major political systems are different, however, because the transports to be attacked demand different tactics. Memory must be fought with a false history made so ubiquitous that what scattered individuals remember can only seem fleeting and insubstantial when faced by the collective memory of the indoctrinated younger generation. Imagination, on the other hand, must be attacked at the root: it must not be given *time* to take flight, no take-off room. The reduction of round, biological human time to speeding-up mechanical time is almost complete. Digital time is a pulse: by mistaking it for the beating of our own hearts, we mistake the demands of mechanical time for our own. Where does dreaming fit?

The attack on unauthorized memory is waged with words. Imagination must be destroyed by the manipulation of images. This is where the difference between the two empires resides. The couple (US and USSR) have essentially different modes of eradicating dissent. Those differences are their specific sexuality. The genital of Communism is the censor. The Capitalist genital is TV. The two have been actively tangling recently: they want our TV, we want their power to forbid.

Roland Topor

The Proof

RODRIGO REY ROSA

Translated from the Spanish by Paul Bowles

One night while his parents were still on the highway returning from someone's birthday party, Miguel went into the living room and stopped in front of the canary's cage. He lifted up the cloth that covered it, and opened the tiny door. Fearfully, he slipped his hand inside the cage, and then withdrew it doubled into a fist, with the bird's head protruding between his fingers. It allowed itself to be seized almost without resistance, showing the resignation of a person with a chronic illness, thinking perhaps that it was being taken out so the cage could be cleaned and the seeds replenished. But Miguel was staring at it with the eager eyes of one seeking an omen.

All the lights in the house were turned on. Miguel had gone through all the rooms, hesitating at each corner.

God can see you no matter where you are, Miguel told himself, but there are not many places suitable for invoking Him. Finally he decided on the cellar because it was dark there. He crouched in a corner under the high vaulted ceiling, as Indians and savages do, face down, his arms wrapped around his legs, and with the canary in his fist between his knees. Raising his eyes into the darkness, which at that moment looked red, he said in a low voice: If you exist, God, bring this bird back to life. As he spoke, he tightened his fist little by little, until his fingers felt the snapping of the fragile bones, and an unaccustomed stiffness in the little body.

Then, without meaning to, he thought of María Luisa the maid, who took care of the canary. A little later, when he finally opened his hand, it was as if another, larger hand had been placed on his back—the hand of fear. He realized that the bird would not come back to life. If God did not exist, it was absurd to fear His punishment. The image, the concept of God went out of his mind, leaving a blank. Then, for an instant, Miguel thought of the shape of evil, of Satan, but he did not dare ask anything of him.

He heard the sound of the car going into the garage over his head. Now the fear had to do with this world. His parents had arrived; he heard their voices, heard the car doors slam and the sound of a woman's heels on the stone floor. He laid the inert little body on the floor in the corner, groped in the dark for a loose brick, and set it on top of the bird. Then he heard the chiming of the bell at the front door, and ran upstairs to greet his parents.

All the lights on! exclaimed his mother as he kissed her.

What were you doing down there? his father asked him.

Nothing. I was afraid. The empty house scares me.

His mother went through the house, turning off lights to right and left, secretly astonished by her son's fear.

That night Miguel had his first experience of insomnia, a word he had never heard. For him not sleeping was a kind of nightmare from which there was no hope of awakening. A static nightmare: the dead bird beneath the brick, and the empty cage.

Hours later Miguel heard the front door open, and the sound of footsteps downstairs. Paralyzed by fear, he fell alseep. María Luisa the maid had arrived. It was seven o'clock; the day was still dark. She turned on the kitchen light, set her basket on the table, and, as was her custom, removed her sandals in order not to make any noise. She went into the living room and uncovered the canary's cage. The little door was open and the cage was empty. After a moment of panic, during which her eyes remained fixed on the cage hanging in front of her, she glanced around, covered the cage again and returned to the kitchen. Very carefully she took up her sandals and the basket, and went out. When she was no longer in sight of the house she put the sandals on and started to run in the direction of the market, where she hoped to find another canary. It was necessary to replace the one which she thought had escaped due to her carelessness.

Miguel's father awoke at quarter past seven. He went down to the kitchen, and, surprised to see that María Luisa had not yet come, decided to go to the cellar for the oranges and squeeze them himself. Before going back up to the kitchen, he tried to turn off the light, but his hands and arms were laden with oranges, so that he had to use his shoulder to push the switch. One of the oranges slipped from his arm and rolled across the floor into a corner. He pushed the light on once more. Placing the oranges on a chair, he made a bag out of the front of his bathrobe, dropped them into it, and went to pick up the orange in the corner. And then he noticed the bird's wing sticking out from under the brick. It was not easy for him, but he could guess what had happened. Everyone knows that children are cruel, but how should he react? His wife's footsteps sounded above him in the kitchen. He was ashamed of his son, and at the same time he felt that they were accomplices. He had to hide the shame and the guilt as if they were his own. He picked up the brick, put the bird in his bathrobe pocket, and climbed up to the kitchen. Soon he went on upstairs to his room to wash and dress.

A little later, as he left the house, he met María Luisa returning from the market with the new canary hidden in her basket. She greeted him in an odd fashion, but he did not notice it. He was upset: the hand that he kept in his pocket held the bird in it.

As María Luisa went into the house she heard the voice of Miguel's mother on the floor above. She put the basket on the floor, took out the canary, and ran to slip it into the cage, which she then uncovered with an air of relief and triumph. But then, when she drew back the window curtains and the sun's rays tinted the room pink, she saw with alarm that the bird had one black foot.

It was impossible to awaken Miguel. His mother had to carry him into the bathroom, where she turned on the tap and with her wet hand gave his face a few slaps. Miguel opened his eyes. Then his mother helped him dress and get down the stairs. She seated him at the kitchen table. After he had taken a few swallows of orange juice, he managed to rid himself of his sleepiness. The clock on the wall marked quarter to eight; shortly María Luisa would be coming in to get him and walk with him to the corner where the school bus stopped. When his mother went out of the room, Miguel jumped down from his chair and ran down into the cellar. Without turning on the light he went to look for the brick in the corner. Then he rushed back to the door and switched on the light. With the blood pounding in his head, he returned to the corner, lifted the brick, and saw that the bird was not there.

María Luisa was waiting for him in the kitchen. He avoided her and ran to the living room. She hurried after him. When on entering the room he saw the cage by the window, with the canary hopping from one perch to the other, he stopped short. He would have gone nearer to make certain, but María Luisa seized his hand and pulled him along to the front door.

On his way to the factory where he worked, Miguel's father was wondering what he would say to his son when he got home that night. The highway was empty. The weather was unusual: flat clouds like steps barred the sky, and near the horizon there were curtains of fog and light. He lowered the window, and at the moment when the car crossed a bridge over a deep gully he took one hand off the steering wheel and tossed the bird's tiny corpse out.

In the city, while they waited on a corner for the bus, María Luisa listened to the account of the proof Miguel had been granted. The bus appeared in the distance, in miniature at the end of the street. María Luisa smiled. Perhaps that canary isn't what you think it is, she said to Miguel in a mysterious voice. You have to look at it very close. If it has a black foot, it was sent by the Devil. Miguel stared into her eyes, his face tense. She seized him by the shoulders and turned him around. The bus had arrived; its door was open. Miguel climbed onto the platform and looked behind him. "Dirty witch!" he shouted.

The driver started up. Miguel ran to the back of the bus and sat down by the window in the last row of seats. There was the squeal of tires, a horn sounded, and Miguel conjured up the image of his father's car.

At the last stop before the school the bus took on a plump boy with narrow eyes. Miguel made a place for him at his side.

"How's everything?" the boy asked him as he sat down.

The bus ran between the rows of poplars, while Miguel and his friend spoke of the vast power of God.

Mission

NADJA TESICH

I was in the public square of a small town without knowing what would happen next. It was a summer day, August or July, late afternoon, shadows stretched. I could see him in the distance across the square but he kept fading in and out, his form just a bit of color, red. In the bag I find a comb and mirror, then comb my hair, will he turn and look now, no he has gone away. I sit by the fountain, the shadows get taller, what next?

Then the church clock struck six, very slowly it went like death, killed every other sound in the place and that was a signal between us—he had to be back by six or something went wrong and I should look for him fast. I don't want to do that, I don't know this place. Should I run away? Where to? In the square, total emptiness, nobody but me and the sound of water at my back. Where he used to be on the other side I see something move slowly then I see a cat. I'd better wait another five minutes just in case the clock is wrong. What if we miss each other along the way? Where is my watch? My hand is red with long filthy nails but the watch isn't there, must have left it by the bed, a stupid thing to do since you can't trust the church clocks.

I waited. A dog came over, frightened me, he is very big. I am afraid of dogs. This one is lazy and old. He sits down next to me, closes his eyes. Maybe he will not bite. I heard a window shutter open. A woman appears, shakes out some sheets. She has long black hair, she hums a bit then goes inside. Everything is empty again until a gypsy woman arrives with a kid. She'll ask for something I think. I check my bag. Everything is there. I put it on my back. The gypsy woman only stops at the fountain, gives some water to the kid, then moves away toward the church.

The church clock looks like a spider, on it it says six fifteen. It's time to look for him, can't wait. I circle the square first then take a side street left, the direction he was supposed to take. What if I am late? I should go faster. Maybe run. I run fast. My bag is heavy on my back. Suddenly a large crowd fills the street, some sort of dancers, singers, acrobats. They spilled everywhere, into other side streets, is it the end of the corrida or what? I was going against the current, can't go fast, keep bumping into them. I thought I saw him once way ahead but it could have been someone else. I only saw his back. I can't keep going like this, what if the direction is wrong, what if I miss him? The only thing to do is ask, had they seen him maybe, maybe someone has. Have to do it even if it's wrong. But they only shrugged their shoulders and answered briefly in a language I didn't understand. I realized that I had difficulties describing him well. The words I used didn't correspond really to what I wanted to say. It was like describing color or smell. I had never seen him that well. That was the problem.

I kept walking left and right then straight ahead. The acrobats, dancers, magicians are no longer there. It's dark now, all the streets are deserted, only dogs bark. I think about going back to the square but decide against it, it would be irrational. I know that we had agreed on that. Just keep walking, don't look back, they said. I leave the last white house behind, take a path and suddenly I am by the road at the edge of town, barely visible now except for the church top. Had I walked the whole night? It must be five a.m. judging by the color of the sky. It's early, will have to wait a couple of hours before some car picks me up. I look for my bag but it's no longer on my back. Panic enters me, what next? The road is in front of me, it extends right and left—which direction to take, I no longer have a map. I hear my heart now, as loud as that clock, pointless to cry, think fast. I realize I had been on that road before with the same church steeple, recognize it now in the dream, that time of my life, but the memory is too clear, too sharp, the pain of it wakes me up.

I wait like that by the road, not in the dream but in Spain, maybe the whole night. I go across to the other side of the road where the church steeple is no longer seen. It's very late and dark yet I feel safer with shrubs than on the street inside the town. When I wake up next to a cypress tree, it's cold, must be five o'clock. I look for my watch, it's not on my wrist, did I lose it last night? It's in my bag, can't remember why I took it off. It says five ten, it still ticks. It's cold, I shiver, my stomach growls. My hands are an ugly red color, too much sun. What next? Wake up! From now on, I am on my own—this part was never planned, me and whatshisname were to leave together, either he or one of his people were to take me to a town with a train station. He was to give me something too, our exchange never took place, what to do with the stuff inside my bag? Destroy it? What if I am wrong? They said nothing about it, it was all supposed to end well. I should have asked more questions, my fault. Think fast! Make a fire and burn them up maybe, would they go up in flames, not a chance, too thick, too solid and besides, I don't have a match. I should have brought matches. Maybe go back, try to find the house where I spent the night, ask them what to do next. Which is better—to go there or to burn them, a hypothetical question since I don't have matches. And it's against the rules—whatever you do they said, keep going, don't go back. Not after the exchange. To shred them would be the best but how do you shred this many passports with only a pen knife. It seems such a waste to destroy them, all the work it took with photos and the rest. Months of work. This part wasn't planned, how do I know what's best. I am on my own, have to get back somehow. The hell with the passports! The main thing is to escape. Can't be caught with the evidence on me. God, what if I am caught! Don't think about it. Well, right or wrong, something has to be done. I wish I had some coffee. In Paris now I would be having some croissants and coffee, no in Paris now I would be asleep in my bed. Hell. Useless to think about Paris, get it out of your head! It's quite light now, through the branches I see the town with a bit of mist. I dig a hole next to the tree, I make it big as a grave for a dog or cat then get the stuff from the bag. Brand new passports are in my hand, real faces inside. Better not look at their names, it's just better, you never know what can happen. This way no matter what I can't betray anyone. Even if tortured. No, calm down, everything will end well. I bury them now in one bunch like that, then pile some dirt over, finish it off, one more sweep with a branch, done. Nobody would ever know where they rest. Dead passports under a cypress tree. I try to laugh.

It's going to be cloudy, the sky is the color of lead. I pull out a map, wonder which directions to take, it's best to head north, reach Irun, stay there with friends. They are not really friends, just names on a sheet of paper, friendly people, but not suspected. Category B, very useful, they said. Maybe go to Lerma which is closer, there I could stay with one of those as well. In any case I have to go north which means get out of the forest, cross the road to the other side, head west. It's uncertain, all of this, my first mission, and failed. What could I have done differently, what did I do wrong? Nothing at all. That's a fact. I cross the road and sit on the ground.

There are no cars at all, still too early. My watch says almost six. A bicycle appears and I hide for some reason. Just an old man peddling very slowly. A tourist car would be the best, then I could go north with them, become one of them. Nobody bothers the tourists. Too early for tourists, they must be still asleep or having a nice breakfast. Should I wait for a tourist car or hitch the first ride? These are just thoughts, there aren't any cars. I wish I had something to eat, should have made a sandwich last night, been more prepared. I wish I smoked now, even that would help. I find some gum but it only makes me nauseous. I wind my watch, it's five minutes fast judging by the church clock. I hear murmurs now of the town behind, very faint, they are waking up, then I hear another louder sound, a big heavy one. I see a truck coming from the right, a very sluggish one. Split second decision, go hitch a ride. I wave my scarf. He seems to have seen me before I got up, he started to slow down, maybe he'll turn off, head for the town. No, he stops, picks me up.

A big guy who's maybe not big but hefty is in the truck. He is neither young or old, not handsome or ugly, just an average Spanish guy, sort of dark. I say, "hola," point to the large town ahead on my map, then sit next to him. He moves his head up and down which means yes, it's fine. In front, next to the mirror, he has two small bears that swing. He has a couple of pictures on his side and staring at me a large photo of a pin-up. One of those pink ones from *Playboy* maybe. She doesn't look Spanish, wherever he got it. What if he rapes me, a sudden thought, what is worse, to be raped or caught? Probably to be caught because then they rape you in addition. They do that. Never get caught! Maybe nothing will happen, don't think gruesome thoughts. But how do you stop them? An old superstition is coming back for the first time since eight—if I count to five and he says nothing then everything will be fine, if I count to six and don't see another car then . . . this is silly, my mind has to be sharp, logical, instead of this. I have to try to stay awake but how can I. I feel myself nod. He is silent. Why doesn't he say something, that would be better. When confronted with a dangerous person, it's best to talk, mother said once. I can persuade him not to. Have to establish contact.

He finally says, "Inglesa?" and I say "Si." No point in saying no, we are probably the same to him. My being an American would just cause more confusion in his mind. It's hard to know which ones they prefer. I say "Donde?" and show the map again. He lets one hand fly, "Francia" he says, like it's the end of the world, what a miracle, don't have to catch the train at all. What good luck. "Me too," I say and relax a bit. I know I shouldn't fall asleep but the slow drizzle is doing it to me and those two bears that swing and the windshield wipers. First thing I'll do is shower, the moment I get in, then sleep, maybe call them right away, maybe not. A sudden stop makes me jump. I must have fallen asleep against his shoulder, my God, what he'll think. We are outside some place with blue doors and flowers in front, must be a restaurant. It says 'Angelica' in front. "Café," he says, "vamos," helps me get down, then we go inside. It's a small place, white-washed, has tables with blue oilcloth tops. Two guys sit in one corner, one with a moustache. They look like they drive trucks too, this must be that kind of restaurant. He orders some coffee and an omelette with potatoes inside. I devour mine. The waitress, who is older and dark, looks unfriendly, is she giving me a dirty look? "Hungry," he says to me and winks. I nod yes. He waves again to that woman and motions to my plate. They must be talking about me and how hungry I am. She laughs, seems friendlier when she brings me two sweet rolls. More coffee for both of us. I know I shouldn't offer to pay, not in Spain, they only get insulted. The men here are supposed to be offended easily. The coffee is wonderful, better than any other coffee anywhere. The only problem is that the cups are too small. We have three cups each. Our efforts at communicating are pathetic, mostly a lot of eyebrows and hand gestures. Suddenly I say, "You speak French?" and he says yes he does, but not well. He grins now. I notice his teeth need a lot of help but his French is about a hundred times better than my Spanish. It's not perfect, he is right, but he knows many words, that's enough. His hands are big, hairy, why does he have so many scars? Well, if you drive a truck, that's how it is, don't worry about the scars. I look at my own hands now, they are a sad sight, black nails, all scratched up. I think about the passports and panic swells in me, what if I forgot one? I look around for the bathroom, he seems to stare at my hands. "Lavabo," he says and I find it, a very dirty one for the ladies. I check my bag first. Nothing in it except mine, nothing suspicious at all, no pictures of any sort, even if they search at the border, so what.

When I come out, I see a cop at the next table, not a cop but a *guardia civil*. They are worse. My whole body pulls back, tightens in shock, what's going on? I should really look at him, smile, be casual, like a party. He looks directly at me. My hair is too blond. It attracts attention in Spain, it should have been dyed. They argued to the contrary—that my tourist looks are perfect, will protect me, you don't imagine an American student doing anything subversive. I smile at my shoes, go back to my seat. My driver isn't there, probably went to pee. The cop's eyes hover around my temples, I feel them in profile. He makes me feel like a victim, not a good thing, mother always said even dogs can tell if you are afraid. I am not a victim, straighten up! I could have said no when it was assigned to me. Nobody forced me. They had their reasons when they chose me, but why it should be a girl is no longer clear. Was it ever? The clothes were perfect, that I know for certain, not too flashy or too poor, respectable enough, the looks of a student or an *au pair* girl, a nice girl like in my passport picture. Two years ago. Now they are all crumpled up, smudged with dirt, but my hands are clean. My driver appears from the bathroom, pays the woman, motions to me. Then suddenly stops to talk with the military guy. They seem friendly, what is he telling him now? I can't hear it well. It's probably nothing, just something casual like 'how's your truck' or your football team. You can't panic every second and have morbid thoughts. Don't look curious either, look nonchalant. Comb your hair, look like a coquette! The driver points toward the sky, makes a gesture of disgust. The cop looks buddy buddy with him then winks at me. He probably thinks the truck driver picked me up. We get into the truck.

I feel much safer inside but it's only an illusion of safety, what if he said something to that cop. You never know, you just can't and I can't ask him in French 'what did you talk about?' I shouldn't even mention the cop. An innocent American girl would never worry about the cops. She wouldn't even know anything about Spain and besides, our government is on their side. He seems distant now, something about his mood is different, the way he drives. Am I imagining it? Probably. The rain is doing it to him, he is tired. He was more human inside. IF CAUGHT DENY EVERYTHING! THEY HAVE NOTHING ON YOU! JUST GET ACROSS. It will happen, it's not far. This wasn't planned at all. I am on my own. Hell. WHAT IF HE BETRAYED ME, WHAT IF HE HAD SOMETHING, WHAT IF HE HAD MY NAME? No, he didn't have my name. I didn't have his either. They thought it was best that way. DID HE HAVE MY PICTURE? MAYBE HE HAD IT. No, he had nothing at all. He was to recognize me by the red scarf on my head, wear it first, they said, then once you see him put it around your neck. I examine the scarf now, it's more burgundy, bright red seemed too vulgar somehow. I don't like bright red. WHAT IF HE WASN'T THE RIGHT GUY, WHAT IF THE RIGHT GUY NEVER CAME, WHAT IF THE COLOR WAS WRONG. No, everything was fine. Our signals worked even though he seemed far across the square. I go over it step by step, everything I did was according to the rules: I arrived, I saw him, I signaled, he answered back with his hat, then he was to go inside the town, not far, then come back. He was to reappear exactly at six and I would follow him, always at a distance, toward a house, not the one last night but another one. Everything was to be done before six for some reason, then he would leave right away, take me to the town with the train station. Either he or someone else. He never came back. Not the second time. I allowed an extra fifteen minutes even though they said leave at six sharp. I figured I would give him extra time, in Spain they have different ideas about time. The train for Paris leaves around nine, I remember now, that's why they figured we should be done by six o'clock.

"You like Spain?" he says in French.

"Yes, very well."

"Next time you come, you speak Spanish," he says.

"Yes," I say. It would certainly help. What a dumb idea to send someone inside Spain without knowing the basics. It doesn't fit. Why didn't I ask questions like that in Paris. It seemed awkward then, proof that you were trying to get out of it. A car took me to Irun, then another Spanish one to Tula and I would take the train back. They thought this was best.

"You study here, you study Spanish?"

"No, I visit," I say very slowly and cheerfully. It's obvious I don't study Spanish.

"Very nice," he says. "You have Spanish friends."

Is that a question? "Yes, it is," I say, "many friends everywhere in Spain."

"In Madrid," he says, "your friends?"

"I have friends in Madrid, in Barcelona, in Irun," I brag, "many friends." We sound like Indians in the movies.

"You want to stop in Irun when we come, you see your friends, no? I have friends in Irun. Cousin."

"Maybe," I say, "but I'd rather go to France. You drive to France?"

"Yes, I drive, but we stop in Irun. I eat, you see a friend. I see my cousins." All I want to do is get across and now he wants to see his relatives. Obviously I can't seem too eager or frightened or try to push him too hard.

"Maybe," I say. "I am tired. I'd rather go back."

"Not good for girl to travel like this," he gestures with his thumb. "No good. Next time you take train, no. In Spain nice girl never travel that way." What is he leading up to with this 'nice girl'? He is married, judging by his ring, but it doesn't mean a thing. Some of those are the worst.

Yes," I say, "I was going to take the train . . . " I stop. I had gone too far.

"You change your mind, no?"

"We broke up," I say like a fool and the nerves do the rest. "He fell in love with someone else."

He laughs. What a mistake. Now he'll think I am available to him.

"Don't worry. You find another. Pretty girl. Spanish?"

"I don't understand."

"The fiancé."

"Oh him, yes."

"And you come to see his family in Tula, right?"

This is a trap, the next thing he'll want to know his name and the family name, all of them know each other in Spain, everybody is cousin or second cousin, think up a name for my fiancé. "Yes," I say, "his family, very nice."

"You go to Tula, you meet parents. Too bad. And the name?"

"My name?"

"Family in Tula."

"Santamarina," I say, "you know them?"

"Many families with that name in Tula." I'd better think up a first name, my friend Carlos in Paris, no better not use his name at all, he is Santamarina. My driver is too much of a gentleman to ask me for his first name I guess.

"You meet in England?"

"No, in Paris. He studies in Paris."

"Why, Madrid no good?" This one is a real chauvinist.

"He wanted to get away from his family, you know, to be on his own."

"Family opposed?"

"My family, so-so."

"No. Santamarina family cause problems. That's why you break up."

"Oh no, not them," I say. "They are very nice. He just changed his mind."

"Probably family," he says. "They want Spanish girl. I know. They think foreign girl is not nice." There he goes using again that word 'nice.' "You like it in Tula?"

"Very much. Nice church," I say, how dumb, what else can I say. I saw nothing, can't even talk about bullfights.

"You see the corrida, right?"

"Just one." In Spain they laugh if you tell them you are terrified.

"You like?"

"Very interesting." From what I know the bull has no chance, none. "Do they kill them every time?" I ask casually.

"They try," he says and smiles. I don't like the way he said that. Something about it is wrong and here I briefly thought he was a nice guy. He drives and drives, silent again with those two bears and a pin-up. Then he turns the radio on for a while. To make things worse, a whole truckload of soldiers passes us. They sit all in green with guns pointing up. I feel myself slide into my seat.

Another truck full of them and another. The last one is a jeep full of green-looking officers. My driver waves to them happily as if they were his cousins. You can't deny the evidence, you'd better face the facts—my luck to get into a truck with a Franco guy. But it's safer, much better this way, think how they'll laugh in Paris.

"In Tula they have problems. You know?"

"Problems? I don't understand."

"Last night. Your family tell you, no?" What is he talking about?

"I sleep last night," I say. "Too upset about Juan."

"Juan," he says, "who is Juan?"

"My fiancé, we broke up. I am sad."

"They say nothing?"

"About what?"

"They catch somebody," he says, looks directly at me, oh my God, everything is clear, they talk with the cop, he is probably one of them, just pretends he is driving a truck. He has nothing on me, zero. And I have no interesting information to tell him, even if I wanted to. But this guy they caught, is it possible?

"What did he do, a thief?"

"If they catch him, he did something," he says, very sly.

"You read it in the paper?" I say and this makes him laugh.

"Not in paper, not on TV," he says and laughs again, shows those ugly teeth. "What you think of Spain?"

"Very beautiful," I say, trying to sound as if I am cheering for some football team.

"How we live, you like, what do you think?" Why doesn't he come out and ask plainly what I think about Franco. Well, buddy, you won't catch me now, I know your sign.

"I don't know much about Spain," I say. "Only from books. I read Hemingway, you know, bullfights."

Hemingway sends him into a total fit. "Hemingway," he repeats, laughs, then suddenly gets mean. "Students are stupid," he says. "Police is right." He is shouting as if I did something to him. Why do they hate students everywhere, you can't get away from it, in Spain or America. Jealousy, it's obvious.

"Some students are OK," I say, trying to keep up the conversation. I don't like it when he gets silent.

"No," he shouts. "Not good. Stupid. To be caught in front of church, in the plaza, is dumb," he shouts, demonstrating with his head and fingers how dumb.

"I see," I say. "They caught a student in Tula."

"Yes, in Tula last night. Me, never be caught like an animal in the plaza," he says and laughs for some reason. Well, there it is. How many students could you have in Tula, in the square. He is caught, damn him, did he ignore the instructions, what was he doing on the square? Was he looking for me? It's a question of time before they get me. Will he talk? But wait, maybe this is a different case altogether, I had no idea the guy was a student.

"They say he was with others, French," he says. "Policeman told me." He isn't even trying to hide any more but why does it sound like he isn't sure of all the facts.

"What do they do with him?" I ask.

"You never know what they find. Students are dumb. They do stupid things."

"And the French, they catch them?"

"Not yet," he says. "They catch a gypsy woman with a child." That makes him roar with laughter again.

"What gypsy woman, there was no gypsy woman," I hear myself say in English. I actually hear my words. He didn't understand a thing, thank God, didn't even turn his head. "Why a gypsy?" I ask to cover up.

"Why not," he says and laughs sadistically.

"How much longer to the border," I say after a while.

"Not far. We stop in Irun and you see friends, no?"

"We don't have to," I say.

"It's good to see friends. It's better."

"I'll see them next time. They are only friends of friends. Next time."

"What is the name?"

"Whose name?"

"Friends in Irun," he says like a real cop.

"It's a hard name to say," I answer and start searching for the paper. If I don't tell him, and we get there and I have no friends, it's worse, and all the names on the list are okay, safe, I was told never to hide them. It's better that way. If he is a cop he'll just get reassured that I am visiting nice people, all lawyers, doctors, family men. I try to read the name in Irun from the paper but it's a hard Basque name. He seems impatient, snatches it from my hand then having read it puts it in his pocket. This is something I didn't expect.

"Okay," he says, "we don't go to Irun." Why the sudden shift like that? "We go and talk somewhere else." I don't like this talk, I have talked enough. Did he talk, I wonder about the man who was caught. Will they make me talk? Is he taking me to the police station, why didn't he do it earlier, he could have done it in that restaurant. It must be that paper with the names of those people in Irun, maybe the cops know all of them but then why did they give it to me? My only link with them is that paper, I have to get it back flush it down the toilet. I mention having to go to the bathroom but he ignores me. I have to ask for my paper.

Suddenly he turns off the main road and starts going somewhere else. I look at the map, don't see the road he is on. Houses have disappeared, there is nothing around but drizzle and those two bears. He has turned the radio on again, horrible martial music blares. I am changing my mind, no he isn't a cop, just a sympathizer. He isn't taking me to the station or he would head for a town, it's obvious he'll just pull off the road into the woods and rape me. What else could he want. I have no money. He is mumbling things to himself.

"How old?" he says.

Me?

"Twenty-two," I say, which makes him laugh again. I don't like his teeth or his scars.

"You have kids?" I am trying to appeal to his fatherly side.

"Four," he says but doesn't go into details, just keeps going on that narrow deserted road and suddenly, looking in both directions, he turns sharply and we are in front of a farm house that looks old, deserted, beat-up. And sure enough he says, "We stop now. We talk, you and I."

"No," I say, "I go to France. Or I go to Irun and see my friends. Please give me my names."

"Get out fast," he says, looking around him at the road to see there'll be no witnesses to his crime. "I'm not going," I scream in every language I know. I try to open the window, maybe there's someone in that farm. I hit him with my bag, which only makes him laugh. He says, "Please get out." He is trying to pull me out of the truck by force. I shout, Is there anyone to hear me? He is stronger than me, my only hope is someone will hear, but who, we hadn't passed any cars. In the distance I see a woman leading a donkey or a horse across the field on the other side. I start to shout some more, he reaches and puts his hairy hand over my mouth, pushes me all the way down, is now almost on top of me. "You stay here, good, three or four days, with cousins, then I come back, take you to France. They watch the border now. Everyone is arrested, in Barcelona, in Irun." He lifts his hand off my mouth, looks disgusted. "Why you shout like that," he says. "Stupid students," he starts again, "this one here in Irun is old man, no good, in prison." I want to ask him many questions but my voice isn't there when I try. I start crying instead, very loud, and hate myself. The living proof that I am not made for it is here—I am crying just like a girl in front of this guy. Probably screwed everything up, he got caught and nothing happened to me.

"Not your fault," he says, "no, no, not you. We go in, I explain. Not you. Students." He touches my hair and I sob some more. I love him really, everything, the teeth and his scars, I want to embrace him but it all looks unreal—him, the farm and the woman with the horse in front of us. She stands silent in front of the truck, both her and the horse look alike. Am I dreaming this, I think, if not what will I remember later.

Last Night

FAE MYENNE NG

When Hang Fong Toy finally awakens, she can't tell if the rhythmic pounding is one of her headaches or just the water pipes banging again. She looks around the room, listening. The street light falls through the Venetian blinds; the slanting lines make the room seem larger.

You Thin Toy sleeps curled toward the wall, a brush stroke on the wide bed. He's a retired merchant marine and has sailed the world. Now he spends afternoons at Portsmouth Square, playing chess and telling stories about himself as a young man. "Like a seagull," he says, "I went everywhere, saw everything."

His oldtimer friends like to tease him, "So, why do you sit around the Square now?"

"Curiosity," he says, "I want to see how you fleabags have been living."

You Thin knows all the terms for docking a ship; Hang Fong can name the parts and seams of a dress the way a doctor can name bones.

Hang Fong sews in a garment shop. She's only been outside of Chinatown for official business: immigration, unemployment and social security. When the children were young, they took her to Market Street, the Emporium and J.C. Penny's, but now, without translators, she's not an adventuress.

There was a time when her desire to return to China was a sensation in her belly, like hunger. Now she only dreams of it, almost tasting those dishes she loved as a young girl. Sometimes she says to You Thin before falling asleep, maybe a visit, eh?

After raising their children, Chinatown has become their world. They feel lucky to have an apartment on Salmon Alley. Louie's Grocery is around the corner on Taylor, and Hang Fong's sewing shop is just down the block. Their apartment is well situated in the back of the alley, far from the traffic fumes of Pacific Avenue.

Hang Fong and You Thin like their landlord, an old Italian lady, and her mute son so much that they have given them Chinese names. Fay-Poah (Manager Lady) and Ah-Boy (Mute-Son). Manager Lady wears printed pastel dresses that Hang Fong, a sewing lady, admires very much. Ah-Boy, a big man with a milky smell, works as a porter at the Oasis Club, but during the day he works around the building. When Hang Fong hears his broom on the stairs or the garbage cans rattling in the airshaft, she feels safe. It's good to have a strong man like Ah-Boy nearby. She tells You Thin, Ah-Boy is a good son, and You Thin nods. He likes to think that the anchor tattoo on Ah-Boy's arm makes them comrades of sorts.

Hang Fong thinks, maybe Manager Lady left her window open. But then the sound becomes erratic and sharp. Hang Fong gets up, leans toward the wall. You Thin lets out a long breath.

Hang Fong presses her ear against the wall, listening. Her eyes are wide open. Suddenly she rushes toward her sleeping husband and shakes him, "Get up! Get up! It's the Manager Lady, she's in trouble!"

You Thin stretches out and props himself up on one elbow. He rubs his eyes, trying to wake up. The banging comes again; and the old couple stare at each other. Outside, a car screeches to an urgent stop. They listen to the faint bubbly hum of the fish tank in the other room, and then hear the rumbling ice box motor shut off with a final click. You Thin and Hang Fong look at each other, the silence feels big.

The pounding comes again. Once. Twice.

"Something's wrong! Manager Lady is trying to tell us that!" Hang Fong throws off her covers. In one motion, her legs whip out and her slippers make a swishing noise as she moves across the room. The overhead fluorescent light flickers and snaps and then is quiet. The room is bright, glaring.

You Thin squints, reaches over, and raps sharply, one-two-three on the wall.

A sound knocks back in return.

Hang Fong slaps the wall with her open palm, the sound is flat and dull. She presses palm and cheek into the wall, and shouts, "Manager, Manager, are you all right? Nothing's wrong, is there?"

"SSHHH!!!" You Thin yanks her away.

"Don't talk loud like that, she don't know what you say, maybe she thinks that you yell at her."

You Thin is out of bed, pacing. Hang Fong remains sitting, she pulls her sweater closer around her neck, the sleeves hang limply at her sides.

"Let's see . . . wait a minute, where's Ah-Boy?"

"It's Tuesday, he's got the night shift."

"Oh. Tuesday. Right."

Last week, when You Thin was at Manager Lady's paying the rent, he looked out her kitchen window while waiting for her to come back with the receipt. He saw a Chinese pot beneath a pile of chipped plates. So, the next day, he returned with a blue vase, its floral pattern similar to many of Manager Lady's dresses.

"I see?" he asked, pointing out the window.

Manager Lady opened her mouth wide, as her hand fluttered toward the window.

"Oh. *Si, si*," she said.

You Thin pulled the window open. He moved the cream-colored plates and lifted the pot for Manager Lady to see. She nodded, cradling the blue vase to her bosom.

With two hands, You Thin carried the pot across the hall. Under the running faucet, Hang Fong scrubbed hard. Red, green and yellow, the palace ladies and plum blossoms came clean. You Thin scraped away the last of the dirt with a toothpick. The characters came clear. Good Luck and Long Life. You Thin and Hang Fong laughed, feeling lucky.

"Worth a lot of money, in time," You Thin said.

"Something to pass on to the children," Hang Fong added.

You Thin told everyone on the Square that the pot belonged to a hardworking old-timer who died alone. Hang Fong said that it was a good omen that they were chosen to house this valuable object. "It's very old," she told her sewing-lady friends.

"So, should we call the Rescue Car?" Hang Fong asks.

You Thin looks out the window, distracted. He shakes his head, ". . . but even if they get here in two minutes, best we could do is stand in front of the door with our mouths open."

Hang Fong knows that he wants to climb the fire escape and get inside Manager Lady's apartment. It's risky, she thinks. You Thin isn't a young man and his step isn't always steady. She won't say anything, because the long years of marriage have taught her one thing, he likes his way.

"Well, what do we do?" Hang Fong asks. On the fire escape, a pigeon sleeps, its beak in its chest feathers. Hang Fong watches it. She hears the big engines of the garbage trucks churning up the hill. Fog horns sound in the distance, like help on the way.

You Thin asks, "Well, you think I could make that big step across to their fire escape?"

Hang Fong shrugs her shoulders. "Don't know, how do you feel?"

You Thin raises the window, looks out and snaps back in. Before Hang Fong can speak, he's run to the bathroom and clattered his way out carrying the long wooden board they use as a shelf over the bathtub.

"This is how . . . " He slaps the board. "This will reach from our fire escape to theirs. You hold this end, just in case, and the rest I can do."

Hang Fong grips hard, but she keeps a harder eye on him. Inside, she repeats over and over, "Be careful . . . be safe . . . be careful . . . be safe . . . " You Thin is a brave man, she thinks, You Thin is a good man.

One leg, then the other, and he is over there. He peers through the window, knocks, and then tries to lift it open. Shut tight, he has to pull hard, two, three times before it comes open.

You Thin feels along the wall for the light switch. All along the way, he speaks to Manager Lady, softly, in Chinese, "You're all right, nothing's wrong, don't be frightened . . . " You Thin believes in the power of the voice: a well-meaning word spoken in the face of ill-fortune can turn luck around.

Manager Lady is a wide figure on the floor. Everything around her speaks of her age: the faded covers, the cluttered nightstand, the bottles of lotions and pills. You Thin takes her hands; he's happy hers are warm.

Hang Fong knocks in quick, urgent raps, and You Thin opens the door for her. She moves quickly through the entryway, kneels and takes Manager Lady's head onto her lap, whispering, "Don't be scared, don't be scared." Manager Lady's eyes open; she says something in Italian, the long vowels reach forth and hang heavy in the air. Hang Fong and You Thin look at each other. They understand.

You Thin says, "I go. Go to get Ah-Boy."

"You know where it is then?"

"Uh, let me think . . . where Lee's Rice Shop used to be?"

"No! Across from Chong's Imports."

"Yes, right, I know, I know."

The air outside is sharp. The street lamps cast an orange glow to the empty alley. You Thin moves quickly through Salmon Alley. But when he turns onto Pacific, he rests a moment, the long road before him is marked with globes of light. He runs his hand along the walls for support. On the steep hill, his legs feel strangely heavy when they land on the pavement and oddly light when they bounce off. He chants to himself, "Hurry. Important. Faster."

When he reaches Powell, he leans against the fire hydrant for a moment, glad that he's halfway there. He can see Broadway, it's still brightly lit. He's breathing hard by the time he gets to The Oasis. This late, it's been long closed. You Thin stands outside, banging on the big wooden doors and rapping on the windows. He cups his hands to the barred window, trying to see in. But with the glare from the street lamps, it's like looking into a mirror.

He takes a deep breath, "Ah-Boy, AAHHH-Boy-AAAHH! . . . "

Silence. Then the sound of flapping slippers, and Ah-Boy opens the door, mop in hand.

You Thin throws his arms about, waving toward Pacific. He slaps the restaurant wall, shouting, "Mah-mah, Mah-mah. Be sick. Be sick."

Ah-Boy opens his mouth; his head jerks back and forth, but there is no sound. He lets his broom fall with a clatter. The heavy door slams shut.

Ah-Boy is a big man and You Thin can't keep up for long. At Pacific, You Thin waves him on.

You Thin watches for a moment as Ah-Boy moves up the hill. Yes, he nods, Ah-Boy is a good son.

When You Thin gets to the apartment, Ah-Boy is sitting on the floor with his mother's head in his lap, her gray hair is loosened from its bun. She is speaking to Ah-Boy in a low voice.

You Thin and Hang Fong stand under the door frame, watching. "Just like last year . . ." Hang Fong says, ". . . just like Old Jue."

On the phone You Thin speaks loud. He pronounces the syllables as if each sound were a single character, "Numbah Two. Sah-moon Alley. Old Lady. Sick. You be the come. Now, sabei? I stand by downdaire, sabei? Numbah Two, Sah-moon Alley."

Hang Fong stands next to him, listening hard. She whispers something to him.

You Thin raises his head, and speaks even louder. "One minute. You know, Old Lady, she be . . . uh, uh . . . Old Lady she be come from Italy. You sabei? Lady not from China."

At the Square the next day, You Thin challenges the Newspaper Man to a chess game. You Thin plays with one leg raised on the cement stool. "My Car over your lousy paper Gun, and you're eaten!" The Newspaper Man's children fold *The Chinese Times* on the next table. Lame-Leg Fong tries to tell You Thin which pieces to move. The #15 Kearney bus inches down Clay, its brakes squeaking and hissing. Cars honk.

You Thin tells his story about last night in between chess moves. He describes the distance between Salmon Alley and Broadway. His running motions make his blue sleeves go vlop-vlop in the wind. He repeats all the English words he used, tries to use the ones he'd heard, and makes all the faces Ah-Boy made. He walks the line on the ground to show what he did in midair. Little boys run by on their way to the water fountain.

Hang Fong tells the story without looking up. The ladies listen with rounded backs and moving hands. Sheets of fabric run from the machines to the floor. Clumps of thread knot around the chair legs; spools of color ripple above the ladies' bent heads. The overlock machines click; the steam irons hiss. Some ladies sing along with the drum and gong beat of the Cantonese opera playing on the radio. A voice booms over the intercom system, "LAST CHANCE TO HAND IN THOSE TICKETS, RIGHT NOW!" No one looks up. Some ladies cluck their tongues and roll their eyes. Others shake their heads and curse under their breath.

Many of the sewing-ladies want to hear Hang Fong's story, but missing a sentence here or there, they can't follow the drama. Is it a story or is it real? The women become heavy-footed; the needles stamp urgent stitches into the fabric. Trousers fly over the work tables; the colorful mounds of clothing clutter the floor.

Eventually the grumble of the machines drowns out the story. A young girl runs in to ask her mother for money as the fish peddler arrives, singing out her catch in a breath as long as thread.

FOUR SONGS OF XANADU

Translated from the Chinese by C.H. Kwock & Gary Gach

With the dominance of Genghis Khan, China's poets lost government patronage and began composing new poems to the tunes of popular songs. These Songs of Xanadu, written at the time of Marco Polo and the Crusades, became central in the evolving waterfront theaters.

Kuan Yuan-Shih

to the tune of "A Clear River"

Forsake slight glory
& return
home:
How sweet it is!

A single
laughter
beyond the white clouds.

With bosom friends,
just a few,
—three, four, or more—

To drink like a fish—
There's nothing
wrong with that!

To dance with grand gestures,
stoned,
& complain,
that the world
is too small!

Chiang Kê-Chiu
FROM THE TEMPLE
AT T'IEN-T'AI WATERFALL

to the tune of "The Red Shoes"

Mountaintips
　　　　　in array like
　　　　　　　　swords of snow

Down sheer cliffs
　　　　　streams cascade
　　　　　　　　　curtains of ice.

Swinging through trees
　　　　　wailing gibbons
　　　　　　　　try to grab
　　　　　　　　the tops of clouds.

The cuckoo
　　　　　splatters azalea
　　　　　　　　red with its lament.

The windgod's howl
　　　　　roars from
　　　　　　　　the shadows of caves.

Compared to men's souls
　　　　　mountains
　　　　　　　　are not so dangerous.

Chang Yang Hao
RECALLING THE PAST AT T'UNG PASS

to the tune of "San P'o Yang"

As if gathered together,
        the peaks of the ranges.

As if raging,
        the waves on these banks.

Winding along
        these mountains & rivers,
the road to T'ung Pass.

I look west
        & hesitant I lament

here where
        opposing armies passed through.

Palaces
        of countless rulers
        now but dust

Empires rise:
        people suffer.

Empires fall:
        people suffer.

Anonymous

to the tune of "The Water nymph's Tune"

She waits
      to meet him,
            behind a bower.

In her chamber,
        they fall in each
              other's arms.

Immediately,
       with laughter they tumble
             onto an ivory bed

& speechless
       mumble—
            growing shy with one another.

Stealthy
     & calm, they
          undress themselves.

The red brocade
        quilt coverlet
             pulses in waves.

Gold bracelets
     on her alabaster arms
            clinking chimes

Matching that
     of a drake & his mate
             plashing about.

ALFONSINA STORNI

*Translated from the Spanish by Barbara Paschke
and David Volpendesta*

I. CIRCLE

My chaste and intimate friend gives me her account:
—I'm young, I haven't lived. My husband? A cheat.
I have three children and I see year after year roll
into one, like a dull, emotionless dream.

Tempted, at times I unlock my balcony,
To gaze upon the cultured man, the haughty, the shy.
Useless. If only I could cure myself of this pain!
Ah, love is not a game that relieves anxieties.

It lessens them, perhaps; but men, my friend,
To me are not worth a try;
Their cleverest flattery loosens my besieged heart.

I have a perfect body and a rosy mouth.
I was chosen for the highest love,
But I hide my fire beneath the veil of a nun.

II. THE OTHER FRIEND

Another friend tells me: —We thinking women
Come out losers in the business of love.
Of course, we have many admirers:
They seek little tastes in fallen virgins.

They don't put their hearts in spiritual women
Who fatigue them in the end. Like cultivators

They adore what they create: they think that women
should submit to their own carnal ways.

We thinking women are the bases,
We improve men, and polish their standards,
In us they refine their unleashed instincts.

And when, now tired of waiting, we ask
For their hearts, in exchange for our own which we gave,
She who passes by carries away the ones we adored.

III. AND THE THIRD ONE ADDS

Perhaps she carries him away who costs him least.
In her he found life, so tiresome, more manageable.
Every active mind bears a broken soul
And men, in women, seek a bit of diversion.

The modest woman takes better care of the house
And has no imagined intellectual life.
If she finds herself deceived by the man she adores,
She accepts what's left over and lies down by his side.

That's not why a woman is completely devoted
To the one who without being a lover can be a friend.
Perhaps he too dreams the same dream as we.

And above the daily knot of her peaceful regulated
Life, she guards in her luminous breast
A feminine ideal, of which we are ignorant.

ANCESTRAL WEIGHT

You told me: my father did not weep;
You told me: my grandfather did not weep;
The men of my race have not wept,
They were steel.

Speaking of this, a tear, welling from you,
Fell in my mouth . . . Never have I drunk
More venom from a glass
So small.

Frail woman, poor woman who understands,
Drinking it, I knew the pain of centuries;
O, my soul cannot endure
All its weight!

FORGETTING

Lidia Rosa: today is a cold Tuesday. In your house
Of gray stone, you sleep on an edge
Of the city. Do you still watch over your enamored breast
Although you died of love? I'll tell you what's happening:

The man you adored, the man with cruel gray eyes,
Smokes his cigarette in the autumn afternoon.
From behind the windows he looks at the yellow sky
And the street where faded papers fly.

He picks up a book, goes to the heater,
Sits down, and plugs it in.
And only the noise of torn paper is heard.

Five o'clock. At this hour you fell on his chest,
And perhaps he remembers . . . But already his soft bed
Bears the faint trace of another blushing body.

MUTSUO TAKAHASHI

Translated from the Japanese by Hiroaki Sato

A TALE OF THREE CITIES

Milano   *To Kazuhiko Kumai*

The priestess of Cumae, of Petronio,
dangling in the vacant space of a krater,
replied, "I'd like to die,"
but the sculptor Kumai, in 1986,
seems to tie krater-shaped eternal darkness
to a fleeting band of light, while actually untying it,
and while seeming to untie it, makes a puzzling ring
    by tying it again.
Shall we die, or shall we live?
Ducking in through the ring, or cutting it aside,
a traveler carrying a drawn length of steel: you.
Wrapped things: let them be opened. Or:
Opened things: let them be wrapped. These are
the beautiful magic words of the Mediolanum summer,
the sharp songs of the swallows crisscrossing the evening sky.

Venezia   *To Alex Susana*

This Alexander does not sigh by the Ganges
but enjoys taking walks along the canals of Venezia;
delights not in skillfully riding the stallion of Time
    to create history,
but in walking along the accessories of history;
wanders, an umbrella his stick, in the labyrinth of coincidences
    and inevitabilities, of water and stone,
at times wandering into a forgotten courtyard in a drizzle.
In the courtyard: a bush with no exit; on a wet trunk: the whorl of a snail;
at the end of the labyrinth of existence: a wet, abandoned house,

framed in whose window
are the lagoon of death and the island of death in twilight.
His high window facing the water remains lit throughout the night,
and the tip of his pen keeps spewing blue uncertain water.
But that feeble flow from a corner of his room
falls below through the gutter and fills the canals and the sea of death
with the island of death floating in it—this is also true.

Firenze

To Kimio Kawaguchi

Kimiko fell down the staircase, directly to hell,
Kimio up the staircase to the Renaissance paradise.
But can his pitiful soul bear the terror of renascence?
The rooms upstairs are closed in golden clouds.
Rather than grope the nine heavens in tempera,
go out to the plaza and leave your ass to a chair under the sun.
The red wine of Tuscia is bright, the white refreshing.
This is a lesson not only to the healthy body but to the soul.
The act of copying is, after all, no more than copying of an act.
Break your pencil in two and throw it into the muddy flow from the bridge.
The flow pours on to the sea, the sea never reaches
the shore of your hometown but the terrible precipice at the end of the world.
Straight down the precipice the water falls and, fortunately,
below it, there is no landscape you can paint.

FOR POUND'S GRAVE

Rather than about your grave where laurel trees are planted
on an isle of graves enclosed by a high stone fence,
I'd like to talk about the flow coursing around the isle
    of graves, about the flow of time
moving beyond the pomegranates, elderberries, and sorrels.
You are someone who came from the other shore to this,
someone who, even when alive, could not help thinking
about another shore while standing on one.
We cannot choose the other shore over this
but can only think about another from one.
We come to a shore, drifting.

Roland Topor

ANTONIO PORTA

Translated from the Italian by Anthony Molino

from L'ARIA DELLA FINE

I'm writing to you from the country where
a black hole has replaced our garden of delights
(it was 4 a.m. when the fire started
    when subterranean tongues slit a dull July night)
now a black lake surrounds the crater swamps
the house in a mirror of charred bones
windows open day and night —
here, during the first week in September
the family gathers in memoriam, waiting
for the grapes to be picked
(there was a time when delighted wings
were heard rustling through the park's
centuries, or so we thought
amid cedars under the slender parasols of Roman pines)
and a whale-like magnolia bobs and sways
tossing its leaves to signal the likelihood of change
(things did change) now
the rustling proclaims
the definitive passage
everything is ready — just a slight push
and it's headfirst into the funnel.
I wonder if you if anyone
can understand these words, if the survivors
sitting around the hole
or faraway strangers can...
still, what counts is that I speak to you
breathe
together with those of you I can't see
with all of you,
my friends...

no.45
Sept. 10, 1978

41

dogs sound autumn's alarm
the backs of laborers keep curving
no folk art, just hard work
intense colors on the heated theater's screen
when long restless nights bring
hunters then cawing crows upon us
some people will stir while others stay buried
I don't want to say another word
the time we've got is the time we must use
a few days more before the leaves
turn, and fall —
one last word: work should pacify us
but it doesn't so we start producing dreams.

no. 49
Localitá Cheirasca, Sept. 30, 1978

CESARE PAVESE

Translated from the Spanish by Maggie Leigh

MYTH

The day will come when the young god will be a man,
without sorrow, with the dead smile of the man
who now understands. The sun also passes, distant,
reddening the beaches. The day will come when the god
will no longer know where the beaches of long ago were.

One wakes up one morning to find that summer is dead,
while splendors still storm in one's eyes, as they did
yesterday, and the sun thunders like blood
at one's ears. The color of the world has altered.
The mountain no longer touches the sky; the clouds
no longer pile up like fruit, in the water
a pebble no longer shows through. The body of a man
bends over itself, in thought, where a god once breathed.

The great sun is finished, also the smell of the earth,
and the free road, colored with people
who knew nothing of death. One does not die in the summertime.
If anyone disappeared, there was the young god
who lived for everyone and knew nothing of death.
Over him sadness was the shadow of a cloud.
His step astonished the earth.

               Now weariness
weighs on all the limbs of the man,
without sorrow; the calm weariness of the dawn
that opens a day of rain. The darkened beaches
don't know the youth, who once used to just look at them,
and that was enough. Nor does the sea of the air revive
when he breathes. The lips of the man
turn down, resigned, to smile at the earth.

A MEMORY

There is no man who succeeds in leaving a trace
on this woman. What happened fades in a dream
like a street in the morning, and only she remains.
If it weren't for her forehead touched a moment ago,
she would seem surprised. Her cheeks smile
every time.

       Nor do the days pile up
on her face, to alter the light smile
that radiates on things. She does everything
with hard determination, but it always seems the first time:
yet she lives even the last moment. Her solid body,
her self-engrossed look, give way
to a hushed and slightly hoarse voice; a voice
like that of a weary man. And no weariness touches her.

If you stare at her mouth, she half opens her eyes,
waiting: no one dares to make a move.
Many men know her ambiguous smile
or the sudden frown. If there has been a man
who knows her, moaning, humbled by love,
he's paying for it, day by day, for he doesn't even know
who she's living for today.

       She smiles to herself
her most ambiguous smile as she walks through the streets.

I WILL GO BY PIAZZA DI SPAGNA

It will be a clear sky.
The streets will open
on the hills of pine trees and stone.
The turmoil of the streets
will not change that still air.
The flowers sprinkled
with colors near the fountains
will wink like women
amused. The stairs
the terraces the swallows
will sing in the sun.
That street will open,
the stones will sing,
the heart will beat, gasping
like the water in the fountains—
this will be the voice
that will climb your stairs.
The windows will know
the smell of stone, of the morning
air. A door will open.
The turmoil of the streets
will be the turmoil of the heart
in the bewildered light.

It will be you—still and clear.

MARINA TSVETAYEVA

Translated from the Russian by Nina Kossman

POEMS

All the gold of my hair
Lapses into grayness, meekly.
Do not pity! All came fair,
All inside has merged in singing.

Singing, — distances have merged
In the country chimney's moans.
Lord God! My soul has emerged:
My main and most secret purpose.

1922

●

Do not rush unto me your law.
The law of men is slight.
And please do not paint black the dawn
The color of dove white.

And yet . . . well, if that's what you like!
Though having loved all, true,
When that black day will have to strike,
I'll wake more white than you!

1920

●

The war, the war! The incense at the altars,
The chirring spurs.
But I don't give a damn for the czar's problems
And people's wars.

It's as if on a slightly frayed tightrope
I dance to tiny tunes.
A shadow of someone's shade, I am an idol
Of two dark moons.

1914

●

I know the truth! All previous truths — aside!
No need for humans to fight on the earth with humans!
Look up: it is evening, look up: it is nearly night.
Just what are you all about, poets, lovers, hussars?

Already the dew's on the earth, the wind is low,
The storm of stars in the sky will turn to quiet,
And under the earth we will soon find sleep, we all
Who never let one another sleep above it.

1915

FEDERICO GARCÍA LORCA

Translated from the Spanish by Carlos Bauer

from POEM OF THE DEEP SONG

LANDSCAPE

The field
of olive trees
opens and closes
like a fan.
Above the olive grove
there is a sunken sky
and a dark shower
of cold stars.
Bulrush and twilight tremble
at the edge of the river.
The grey air curls about.
The olive trees
are charged
with cries.
A flock
of captive birds…
that shakes their very long
tail feathers in the gloom.

THE GUITAR

The weeping
of the guitar begins.
Wineglasses shatter
in the dead of night.
The weeping
of the guitar begins.
It's useless
to hush it.
It's impossible
to hush it.
It weeps on monotonously
the way water weeps,
the way the wind weeps
over the snowdrifts.
It's impossible
to hush it.
It weeps for things
far, far away.
For the sand of the hot South
that begs for white camellias.
Weeps for arrows without targets,
an afternoon without a morning,
and for the first dead bird
upon the branch.
O, guitar!
Heart gravely wounded
by five swords.

ANTONIO MACHADO

Translated from the Spanish by Carlos Bauer

THE CRIME TOOK PLACE IN GRANADA

To Federico García Lorca

I

(THE CRIME)

He was seen, walking among guns
down a long street,
going out to the cold fields,
still beneath stars before the dawn.
They killed Federico
when first light appeared.
The squad of executioners
dared not look him in the face.
All shut their eyes;
they prayed: "Not even God will save you!"
Dead fell Federico
—blood on his forehead and lead in his guts.
...For in Granada this crime took place,
understand—poor Granada!—in his Granada! . . .

II

(THE POET AND DEATH)

He was seen walking alone with Her,
unafraid of her reaper.
"The sun already in tower upon tower; hammers
upon anvil," anvil and anvil of the forges.
Federico was speaking,
flirting with death. She listened.

"Because yesterday in my verse, companion,
the blow of your dry palms was sounding,
and you gave ice to my song, and the edge
of your silver sickle to my tragedy.
I'll sing you the flesh you don't have,
the eyes you lack,
the tresses the wind would blow about,
the red lips where they would kiss you…

Today as yesterday, Gypsy, death of mine,
how good to be alone with you
through these breezes of Granada, my Granada!"

III

They were seen walking…
                          Carve, my friends,
out of stone and dream in the Alhambra,
a tomb for the poet,
above a fountain where water weeps
and says eternally:
the crime took place in Granada, in his Granada!

HENRI MICHAUX

Translated from the French by Louise Landes-Levy

IN THINKING OF THE PHENOMENA OF PAINTING

Volition, the death of art.

Drawing without particular intention, scribbling mechanically, almost always faces appear on the paper.

Leading an extremely facial life, one is in a perpetual fever of faces.

As soon as I take a pencil, a brush, one comes to me on the paper, one after the other, 10, 15, 20. And fierce, for the most part.

Are they not simply the perception of my own reverberating brain? (Grimaces of a second face, as when an adult suffers, in shame, to stop crying, and thereby suffers more in his depth, as if he would have stopped grimacing in order to become inwardly more full of grimaces.) Behind the face of motionless characteristics, lonely, a simple mask, another face, superiorly mobile, bubbles, contracts, simmers in an unbearable paroxysm. Behind the congealed features, searching desperately for an outlet, its expressions like a pack of screaming dogs ...

From the brush, good as well as bad, in black blots, they flow, they liberate themselves.

At first one is surprised.

Faces of lost ones, of criminals, neither known nor absolutely strange (strange, distant correspondence!). Faces of sacrificed personalities, of "me's" that life, will, ambition, desire for clarity, for coherency, smother, kill. Faces that will reappear until the end. (It is so difficult to smother, to definitively drown.)

Faces of youth, fears of youth from which one has more or less lost the thread and object, then memory, faces that do not believe that everything has been settled by the passage to adult age, that still fear the terrible return.

Faces of will, that always precede us and tend to preform everything, faces from search and desire.

One leaves the epiphany of thought (one of the numerous that thinking cannot stop from provoking, however useless to intellection, but which one cannot more prevent than valueless gestures at the telephone) ... as if one constantly formed a fluid face in oneself, ideally plastic and malleable, modulated by automation and by an instant synthesis, with the slowness of day and in some way cinematographic.

Infinite crowd, our clan.

It is not in the mirror that one must consider oneself.

Man, look at yourself on paper.

THE BIRD THAT DISAPPEARS

He there, he appeared in the day, the most clear day. Bird.

He flaps his wing, takes flight. He flaps his wing, he disappears.

He flaps his wing, he reappears.

He perches. And then, he is no more. With a flapping of wings, he disappears in the clear space.

Such is my familiar bird, the bird who begins to populate the sky of my small heart. Populate? One will see how …

But I remain in place, contemplate him, fascinated by his appearance, fascinated by his disappearance.

IN TRUTH

In truth, when I say:
    "Great and strong
    Such is death.
    What is living,
    Who made more of it?"
Death, it is I.
In truth, when I say:
    "Don't put parents in your play
    There is no place for them,
    And the woman who gave birth was just at
    the end of her strength,
    Don't ask any more of her,
    Don't make so many scenes,

Unhappiness is altogether natural."
In truth, the woman is not me.
I am the good road that turns back no one.
I am the good dagger that makes two wherever
    I go.
It is I who...
It is the others who do not...

The Vulgarity of Death

On Herbert Marcuse's Death

REINHARD LETTAU

I met Marcuse in June 1967 when he came to Berlin for a visit. From the airport at Tempelhof he drove immediately to the opera where, a few weeks earlier, a student had been murdered by a plainclothes policeman during demonstrations against the visiting Shah of Iran.

On the evening of his arrival he met with a small group of people in his hotel in Dahlem for long discussions. Hans Magnus Enzensberger, Rudi Dutschke, and Henri Lefevbre were there already when I entered the room. The first thing I heard Marcuse say was, "Our dilemma is that the people who would benefit from the changes we wish to bring about do not at all wish those changes themselves." That wasn't exactly what we wanted to hear at that time. Much later he told me how meeting all those demonstrating German students, who were strong antifascists, meant a sort of reconciliation with Germany for him.

Half a year after that evening we found ourselves at the same California university. Marcuse's study was situated two stories above mine, so we saw each other almost daily for over twelve years. He knew no Left "taboos"; for example, he condemned the U.S. attack on Vietnam as much as he attacked the Chinese attack on Vietnam, and he declined an invitation to China with the comment, "I do not go through a door which has been opened by Kissinger!"

Almost all writers and philosophers whom I have met have, in the course of their lives, developed a cunning system of defenses, in order to protect their work from the recurring outrages around them. Not Marcuse. What characterized him was a perpetual vulnerability, his shock, even when face-to-face with the expected, and a daily, painful realization of the context within which he worked. The sentence I heard him say perhaps most often was, "We must do something about this immediately!" He was too sensitive to daily horrors to protect himself from involvement with them. One could say that his work, his writing, had to be done, and defended, in the short intervals of time between each new outrage.

As a child I always thought a philosopher was someone continually astonished by everything, who took everything seriously. Marcuse fulfilled this child-hood notion of mine with his attention not just to ideas, but to everything which could be perceived sensually: a hippopotamus, a head of lettuce, or a teaspoon from his parents' house. These were three objects he loved; while recreational vehicles, portable radios, and motorcycles were three things he hated and wanted to abolish after the revolution. He hated travelling, too, because it meant parting. I loved his respect for objects. He excused the military order in my kitchen with a quotation from Virgil that "things also have tears"; and a right to their own space where they feel comfortable.

He hated death with an intensity that astonished me, until I finally under-stood that only with such a tremendous hatred could one probe the vulgarity, the gratuitousness of death. In December 1972, I invited him and his wife Inge (from whom I learned as much as I did from him) for dinner. He called me the evening before to say she had a stomach ache and could not come. At Christmas-time in Germany, I received a special delivery letter. Marcuse wrote me that Inge was dying of cancer and would have no more than eight months to live. He concluded his letter with the words: " '*L'amour est plus fort que la mort'*—what a disgusting, contemptuous swindle!"

In the last twelve months of his life, Marcuse studied Rudolf Bahro's *Alternative* thoroughly and wrote a profound analysis of it. But, the consequences of public response to "Holocaust," and, in connection with this, the well-known question about the possibility of "poetry after Auschwitz," occupied him most, even to the point of considering a revision of his previous aesthetics. He demanded material, urged discussions, and corresponded intensely about these concerns. He had great difficulties with a literature which, by portraying vio-lence, was a "privatization of Auschwitz"; and he was also disturbed by the new romantic trend in Europe in which there is no more memory of the horror.

His favorite contemporary writers were Peter Weiss and Samuel Beckett, and he felt honored when the latter dedicated a poem to him last year for his eightieth birthday. He asked me a dozen times whether I thought it appropriate for him to write a thank you note to Beckett. I encouraged him, saying that I could not conceive of a writer who would be offended by the fact that Marcuse liked something he had written. He finally did write to him.

Never in all the time I knew him was he so unable to hide his emotion as during our last lunch in La Jolla. He stopped eating and told me that one time Beckett had been asked by a critic to explain the structure of his writing. "I can explain to you the structure of my writing," Beckett answered. "I was once in a hospital and in the room next door a woman, who was dying of cancer, screamed all night. This screaming is the structure of my writing!"

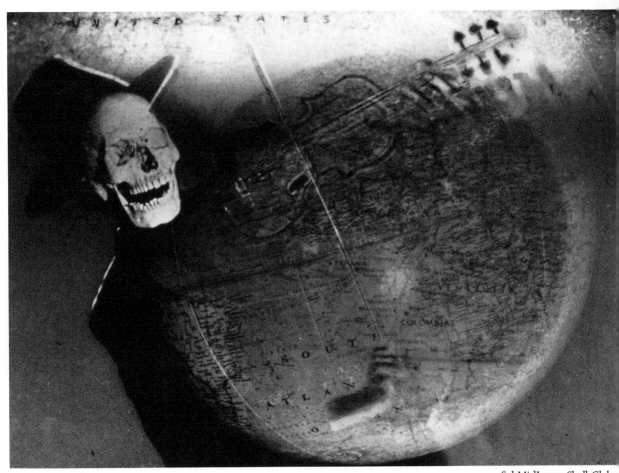

SchMidLapp, *Skull Globe*

The Global Drift
Towards Nuclear War

NOAM CHOMSKY

The National Academy of Sciences has published a study of nuclear and strategic issues. It observes that poll results show that 75% of the American population came out in favor of a nuclear freeze. Of that 75%, some portion knows a freeze is also official Soviet policy. This is probably a small proportion because this policy has barely been mentioned in the American press. Some still smaller portion knows a freeze has been overwhelmingly supported by the U.N. over the rather adamant objection of the U.S. So here we have a situation where 75% of Americans support something, the Soviet Union supports it, most of the world supports it, and still it's not an issue in American politics. It is just not on the agenda in the American political system. And the vast military buildup which was initiated by President Carter, then extended by President Reagan, continues unabated, escalating the already severe threat of a terminal nuclear war. The only detectable effect of the very substantial success of the nuclear freeze campaign is that it did impel the U.S. into negotiations—which were obviously designed to deflect the public's concerns so that the arms buildup could continue without interference. In fact, that's exactly what happened.

Questions About Democracy

This raises some obvious questions about democracy—and other things. A nuclear war is certainly not unlikely. I don't think there's any rational person who thinks it's unlikely—in fact, we've come close to it many times. You might say it's kind of a miracle that we're here to discuss the matter, and it's not too likely that this miracle can persist very long. Just to talk about armaments: the U.S. has approximately 13,000 weapons targeted against the Soviet Union; France and England add about a thousand more and are rapidly increasing their arsenals; the Soviet Union has about 8,500 weapons targeted against the U.S. Of the 13,000 U.S. weapons, about 11,000 are classified as strategic; of those, about half are invulnerable on submarines. Of the 8,500 Soviet missiles, most are land-based, with 95% using liquid fuel. The

Center for Defense Information, from whom I've taken those figures, concludes that despite the numbers, neither country is superior in nuclear weapons. Rather, they say, we are "mutually inferior" since there is no superiority in mutual destruction. I'd say that's a plausible conclusion!

The American government regularly issues warnings which are designed to terrify the taxpayer who has to pay the cost of these military buildups. Sometimes those warnings are on the fanciful side. There was a major interview published in the *New York Times*, with President Reagan and a group of *Times* experts, Leslie Gelb and others, on strategic issues. President Reagan started off by stating, as he has before, that since 1967 the U.S. has been engaged in "unilateral disarmament." He was not called to account for that statement, which is a falsehood so extraordinary that it defies comment. What's interesting is that his interlocutors didn't feel it necessary to say anything about this grotesquely false statement; there was *no* editorial comment. It's considered, apparently, quite appropriate for the President to say we've been engaged in unilateral disarmament during a period when we have been increasing and improving our strategic weapons.

Sometimes these warnings are not fanciful; they are, in fact, quite accurate. Every year the Pentagon puts out a glossy booklet explaining how dire our plight is and how weak we are in comparison with the Russians. In 1983, the booklet actually managed to say something true; it said that the Russians have an ominous advantage over us in liquid-fueled missiles, which is correct—95% of their missiles are liquid-fueled and none of ours are. We abandoned this technology 20 years ago since it was dangerous and unreliable. The booklet didn't go on to say that the Russians have an ominous advantage over us in horsedrawn artillery, but I assume that's also correct—maybe in soldiers without shoes, too.

Recent developments are very ominous. Pershing II missiles in West Germany have a few minutes' flight time to Russian targets. There are Cruise missiles now all over the world—at sea, on land and in the air. They are theoretically undetectable, or will be with Stealth technology. The MX missile, according to Air Force Chief of Staff Lewis Allen, has what he calls "a counterforce first-strike capability." The same is true of the Trident II missiles on submarines.

The effect of all this is well understood, and has been pointed out by any number of people—for example, former Secretary of Defense Robert MacNamara. The effect is to compel the Soviet Union to adopt a computerized response strategy which, of course, increases significantly the danger of war. It means that war can break out by error or inadvertence or technical failure or misassessment of rising international tensions because there isn't any time for human intervention. We know that we also have such systems but fortunately do not rely on them. They have repeatedly failed, and human intervention has aborted programmed nuclear response. The Soviet systems are undoubtedly going to be far worse than ours, and they're going to fail all over the place because their computer systems are more inefficient. What we're doing is increasing the danger that we will be destroyed.

Irrelevance of Public Opinion

What are the reasons for this inexorable drift towards nuclear destruction? What are the reasons for the almost total irrelevance of public opinion or of international willingness to terminate the madness? That's worth thinking about, and that's what I want to talk about. There is a conventional answer—that we have to defend ourselves against a "monolithic and ruthless conspiracy" to conquer the world. In fact, I'm quoting John F. Kennedy at the time when he launched the current phase of the arms race, the huge buildup of nuclear weapons in the early 1960s. Kennedy's "monolithic and ruthless conspiracy," which is supposed to be the source of all trouble in the world, has recently been renamed "the evil empire" by Ronald Reagan, whose policies closely resemble Kennedy's. (That tells us something interesting about the spectrum of American politics, I might add.)

The conventional answer is very uninformative. It carries, in the technical sense of information theory, zero information. The reason is that it's totally predictable: every action of every state is explained on the basis of a defensive need. For example, Hitler would say, when he took over the Sudetenland or attacked Poland, that his actions were justified in terms of the need for self-defense. It was necessary for Germany to defend itself against Polish aggressiveness or against Czech terror against Germans, and so on. And therefore, "What can we do? Everyone's refusing peace, so we are compelled to do this."

Now, there are those people who say Nicaragua is such a threat to us that if Nicaraguans obtain weapons to defend themselves against our attacks against them, we must therefore bomb them. By those standards, Hitler is rather sane, because if Nicaragua is a threat to us, then undoubtedly, Czechoslovakia was a threat to Germany. If you want to evaluate the defensive rhetoric of some state, since defensive rhetoric itself carries no information, what you have to do is look at the historical record to see if in fact they were defending themselves. That's what we have to ask ourselves. Have we indeed been involved in any form of defense over the past years?

After World War II the U.S. was in a position of global dominance that had no parallel in human history. This domination showed up in two dimensions, first in the economic dimension, and second, in the military and strategic dimension. At that time, the U.S. had about 50% of the world's wealth and was responsible for about 50% of the world's production. There's never been a moment like that in history, and American planners formulated policies based on that fact. This is a very open society; therefore, we can find out what they were planning. The documents are available and they are revealing. It's an open society, but that doesn't matter much because nobody looks at the facts! Let's look at them.

To Maintain Disparity

The planning record was pretty much set in the 1940s. What's happened since is an application of the same essentially invariant geopolitical conceptions to various situations, but the basic framework of thinking hasn't changed. Some of the best accounts were presented by George Kennan, one of the most thoughtful and lucid American planners. He's on the dovish, humane side of planning, which makes what he said quite interesting. As head of the State Department Planning Staff in the late 1940s, he produced/wrote a series of papers. One of these, "Policy Planning Study 23" (February 1948) gives an extremely precise and clear account of postwar American foreign policy. Kennan said that we have 50% of the world's wealth and that that disparity creates envy and resentment elsewhere. The primary purpose of our foreign policy, he said, must be to "maintain that disparity." We must abandon "vague" and "idealistic" ideas such as "human rights, the raising of the living standards, and democratization." To maintain the disparity we are going to have to use forceful measures, and "the less we are hampered by idealistic slogans, the better." That's his message and it's correct, accurate, and pointed. It grows out of a geopolitical framework that

had already been elaborately formulated between 1939 and 1945, when American planners met to deal with what they knew was going to emerge from the war—a position of American global dominance. Every rival was being destroyed or severely damaged while the U.S. gained enormously from the war since it was not attacked and the government was able to control a command economy. American industrial production grew by leaps and bounds. Obviously we were going to emerge in the dominant position.

The most interesting of the planning programs was called the War and Peace Study Program, organized by the Council of Foreign Relations, the major business input into foreign policy. It included all the top strategists in the State Department, and the group met for six years to plan out the postwar world. They developed a concept they called "The Grand Area," the area strategically necessary for world control. After a careful geopolitical analysis, it turned out that the Grand Area had to include all the Western Hemisphere, the Far East, the former British Empire, which we were in the process of dismantling and taking over (that's what's called anti-imperialism in American historical writing), and surely the oil-producing regions of the Middle East and Western Europe. That was the minimum Grand Area; the maximum would be everything if we could get it. And, as Kennan later explained as well, the Grand Area has to be subordinated to the needs of the American economy. We have to act forcefully there, without regard for vague and unrealistic notions like human rights, democratization, and raising living standards, because it's going to take force to maintain the disparity.

Remember, that's the message from the liberal, humane side of the spectrum. Kennan was, in fact, removed from the State Department a couple of years later because he was considered too soft, and harder-line people came in. Incidentally, Kennan developed that concept specifically with regard to the Far East, but the U.S. is a global power so its policies are applied everywhere. Kennan himself explained how the policy applied to Latin America in a briefing for Latin American ambassadors held in 1950. He pointed out that one of the main concerns of our foreign policy must be what he called "the protection of our raw materials" (notice "our" raw materials, no mention of "their"). And who do we have to protect our raw materials against in Latin America? No Russians around. We have to protect our raw materials from the indigenous population who might try to threaten the disparity. For example, they might begin to use their resources for their own purposes, and obviously that's intolerable. In fact, anybody who does this is a "Communist," no matter what their beliefs are.

Freedom to Rob

This geopolitical conception remains fixed, and it explains why the U.S. has been so hostile to democratization, higher living standards, and human rights issues, because any move towards those ends is going to be asso-

ciated with limitations on our fundamental freedom—namely, the freedom to rob—and that's the only one we really care about. The freedom to rob has to be maintained; everything else is just rhetoric. Now, countries that move toward their own democratization are going to be concerned about their own populations, and that concern will bring danger to those countries. If you look at historical studies, you won't find this geopolitical doctrine because it's largely suppressed. For example, the best scholarly study of Kennan's influences, as is generally recognized, is John Louis Gaddis's *Strategies of Containment*. In it he claims that Kennan never expressed any geopolitical conception. But Kennan did present such conceptions, such as the ones I've just quoted. However, they're not appropriate for the public to hear. It's of course understood, and need not be said, that scholarship and the media and the schools must continually trumpet "vague and idealistic" slogans about democracy and human rights in an effort to pacify the domestic population, but "serious people" realize such things are going to stand in the way of maintaining the disparity, of subordinating the Grand Area and controlling the world's wealth.

Well, that's the economic side. What about the strategic and military side? Here, too, the U.S. was in a position of enormous power after the Second World War, with no domestic enemies nearby and control of both oceans. There was only one possible threat to American security: ICBMs and thermonuclear weapons—hydrogen bombs. Hydrogen bombs are small and far more powerful than the atom bombs then available. They could be put in the nose cone of a missile and if intercontinental missiles were developed, if hydrogen bombs were developed, then it would be possible for some enemy to threaten us seriously.

Recognizing that, we immediately raise an obvious question—what did American planners do to try to prevent this sole threat to our security? The documentary and historical record contains no indication that any such effort was ever made. It just wasn't an issue. Nobody seemed to care about the development of the only weapons that could possibly threaten the U.S. That teaches us something too. It teaches us that questions of security have never been relevant to the arms race; and they still are not significant. That is why nobody cares. It might have been possible to stop them, possible to enter into negotiations with the superpower enemy that would have blocked the development of those weapons, but nobody wanted to do it. There were other things driving the system, forcing it to go a way in which questions of security were quite irrelevant. That's another observation to add to the matter of the irrelevance of public opinion.

The point remains constant throughout, up until today. For example, take the current idea that Nicaragua is a threat to the United States. The threat is supposed to be that Nicaragua is becoming a Russian base, or that it has Russian weapons—how do we mitigate that threat? The answer is pretty obvious: call off the war against Nicaragua, enter into normal trade relations with it, allow it to proceed with its own programs, at which point it will stop being a Russian base. So we've eliminated the threat. But that idea doesn't cross anybody's mind. The reason is that we want Nicaragua to be a threat. We're trying to drive it to be a Russian base, because that will offer a justification for the use of violence there, which has to be undertaken for other reasons. Since the Nicaraguan government is concerned with the welfare of its own population and it's no longer willing to complement the industrial economies of the West, it is by definition Communist, part of that grim and evil, monolithic and ruthless conspiracy. It doesn't matter if the Russians are there or not; in fact, it would be *better* for us if the Russians were there. Then we would have a reason to carry out the forceful acts that must be undertaken if we're going to maintain the disparity (Kennan's idea). If we're going to insure that the freedom to rob and to exploit is not hampered, obviously we have to be committed to such use of force.

Nicaragua Dominoes

If Nicaragua proceeds with its own programs, then it's not just Nicaragua that's a problem. Rather, the problem is much broader. The geopolitical conception I have been outlining is what is known as the "domino theory." It has two variants: one variant is the kind Ronald Reagan produced when he said that if we don't stop them over there, then they're going to be in Long Beach. That version has been presented by Johnson, by Kennedy, by everyone. We've got to stop them over there or they're going to come over here and rape your grandmother, and that sort of thing. That's one version of the domino theory—everybody laughs about that one and says how ridiculous it is.

However, there's another version that is not ridiculous. It is very sound, it is never challenged, and underlies most American action in the world. The concern is that if some country acts on this terrible concept of using its resources for its own population, and if it works, then there might be a demonstration effect. It might be picked up elsewhere. "The rot will spread"—that's the way the planners describe it, the rot being successful social and economic development outside the framework of control and domination by the U.S. Therefore, we have to stop it. We have to prevent the contagion which is going to infect others, as Kissinger put it when he undertook the overthrow of the Allende government in Chile in the early 1970s. It really ought to be called the "rotten apple in the barrel theory"; one rotten apple may infect them all. That was the original formulation in the 1940s. That makes sense, it fits into the general conception of Grand Area planning and it explains a curious and paradoxical fact about American policy. People are always puzzled, especially Europeans, when the U.S. dedicates itself with such savage feroc-

ity to destroy such tiny, marginal countries as Grenada or Laos. Why was it so essential, let's say, in Laos?

Laos was probably the weakest country in the world; most people in Laos didn't even know they were in Laos, they just knew they were in their village. The first time they knew there was a world out there was when U.S. bombers started coming, driving them into the hills. This was the heaviest bombing in history, exceeded only in Cambodia later on. The American government conceded, quite openly, that this had nothing to do with the war in South Vietnam. It was on its own. The reason was transparent: there was a mild social revolution beginning in Laos, and that was intolerable. There are no resources in Laos that the U.S. cares about. We bombed Laos because the rot might spread. Same with Grenada. As soon as Grenada underwent the Maurice Bishop revolution, we had to destroy it. Grenada has nothing—a little nutmeg, and only 100,000 people—but we had to stop it. The smaller the country, the more dangerous the threat. And that's rational. If other people can think that this nothing little place can do something for its own population with its minimal resources, then they'll think they can do it too. The weaker the country, the worse the threat. So naturally, you have to go after these countries with savage ferocity.

Turn Them into Russian Allies

We want these countries to be threats. We want Nicaragua to appear to be a threat, so Senator Durenburger will be able to pursue his idea that we should invade directly. That's what we have to do to prevent the rot from spreading. If we can't control these countries, can't insure that the freedom to rob is maintained, then we want to turn them into Russian allies. We want them to be Russian bases and we'll attack them until they get Russian weapons in defense (they certainly won't be able to get weapons from our allies), and then we have a justification for overthrowing their governments. This is absolutely consistent, and it happens over and over again. What this indicates once again is that we don't care about questions of national security, or at most care about them marginally. Other things are driving the system, and let's ask what they are.

We have a lot of documentation now from the 1940s about what U.S. planners expected with regard to Europe. At that time they were all screaming about how the Russians were going to take over Europe, but they never really expected a Russian attack on Western Europe at all. The concern was something else; it was national capitalism or socialism or communist participation in democratic politics, all of which could begin to erode the Grand Area and threaten the disparity. That had to be stopped. Our war against South Vietnam was motivated by the same principles; the same is true of our actions in the Middle East and elsewhere. It all follows from the same geopolitical conception.

Let's take a look at the actual military buildup and see what that tells us

about the motivating forces. There have been three major periods in which there have been big military buildups. One was the early 1950s, the second was the early 1960s under Kennedy, and the third is from about 1979 until today—the latter part of the Carter administration and the Reagan years.

The official reason given in the early 1950s was that the Korean War proved that the "monolithic and ruthless conspiracy" was trying to take over the world, so therefore we needed strategic weapons to defend ourselves. There are a number of things wrong with that reason. One is that it's obviously fraudulent since the plans had already been laid much earlier. In fact, the plans appear explicitly in an important internal document called NSC 68, which came out a couple of months *before* the Korean War. This National Security Council memorandum by Paul Nitze detailed why we needed a vast arms buildup. We had to pursue a "rollback strategy," a strategy aimed at breaking up the Soviet Union so we could ultimately incorporate it into the Grand Area, along with its satellites. To carry out this play, we were to introduce "sacrifice and discipline" in the U.S. They said we can't afford to waste resources on consumer goods and can't afford the danger of freedom of speech and debate because we're really at war. They also pointed out that we're vastly stronger than the Soviet Union in any measurable respect—military or economic. But that's not to the point—the Soviet Union was stealing "our" resources, very much the way others in the Grand Area sometimes do, and we had to defend ourselves by a military strategy. The background planning call for tripling or quadrupling the military budget, which was done after the Korean War offered an excuse for it. We were just waiting for an opportunity to carry out plans that were already laid.

The Kennedy Buildup

Let's take a look at the second case, the Kennedy buildup. That was motivated by the famous "missile gap." Now the missile gap was also a fraud. Eisenhower pointed out that during the 1960 election campaign, and the Kennedy people certainly knew it within a couple of weeks after coming into office. Nevertheless, the U.S. proceeded with the buildup of a thousand Minutemen. After the missile gap was conceded to be a fraud, the planned military buildup went on anyway.

What about the third time around? This time it was supposed to be the "window of vulnerability." The President's own commission, the Scowcroft Commission, pointed out that there never had been a window of vulnerability and administration spokesmen are now denying in Congressional hearings that they had ever said there was one. Once again the official reason was withdrawn as fraudulent, but the planned arms buildup went on anyway.

Now it's a fact that big military buildups tend to coincide with an aggressive, adventurist foreign policy. For example, in the early 1950s, the U.S. began the training of Latin American military officers, and that led predictably to a series of military coups. By 1954, thirteen out of twenty Latin American states were under military dictatorships—one concomitant of the big military buildup at home. In 1961, the Kennedy administration made a decision which in terms of its impact is one of the most important in modern history. This decision changed the mission of the Latin American military. (Notice, incidentally, that the U.S. can determine that mission.) From "hemispheric defense," it now became "internal security."

High Tech Torture

Now, hemispheric defense was kind of a joke—there was nobody to defend the hemisphere against except us. However, internal security is no joke at all. Internal security means war against your own population, and that's exactly what happened. Under the impetus of the Kennedy administration, and the Johnson administration that followed, the U.S. backed a war against the people of Latin America on the part of the Latin American military which was being trained and advised by the U.S. So government after government, country after country, fell into the hands of "national security states" modeled basically on the Nazis. They introduced high technology torture and terror and a degree of suppression and violence which a later commission called "a plague of repression"

NUCLEAR WEAPONS REPORT

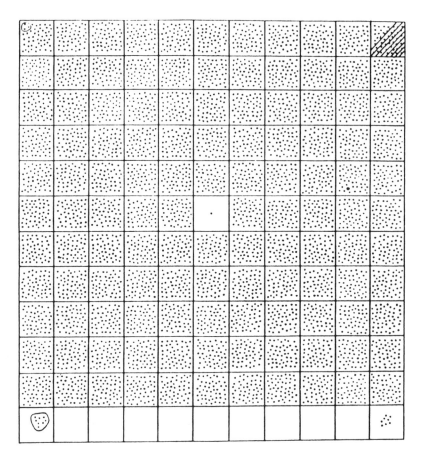

The dot in the center represents all the firepower of World War II—three megatons. The other dots represent the world's present nuclear weaponry, which equals 6,000 World War IIs (18,000 megatons). The US and the USSR share this firepower with approximately equal destructive capacity.

The top left-hand circle, enclosing nine megatons, represents the weapons on one Poseidon submarine—equal to three World War IIs, enough to destroy more than 200 of the largest Soviet cities. The circle in the lower left hand square (24 megatons, eight World War IIs) represents one new Trident submarine with the power to destroy every major city in the northern hemisphere.

Just two squares (300 megatons) represent enough firepower to destroy all the large and medium sized cities in the world.

The amount in the shaded area—100 megatons or less than 1% of the US or USSR arsenal—represents the amount necessary to bring on the "nuclear winter". The dust lofted into the air by the explosion of this small amount would block out sunlight and make temperatures drop so dramatically that our planet would be uninhabitable for plants, animals and humans.

(The chart, which has been reviewed for accuracy by US Senate staff members, appears in *The Trimtab Factor: How Business Executives Can Help Solve the Nuclear Weapons Crisis* by Harold Willens.)

unparalleled in the whole bloody history of the continent.

We had to defend the Grand Area against what in American terminology is called "radical nationalism." That term has a specific meaning which is unaffected by such positions as right, left, center, anything. Radical nationalism means nationalism that doesn't obey American orders, as opposed to moderate nationalism, which is nationalism that obeys American orders. So, naturally we have to block radical nationalism and defend ourselves against it and defend the Grand Area against it. But plainly we're not going to use nuclear weapons against these countries because they're too weak, so why do we need strategic nuclear weapons in the Grand Area?

In National Security Council Document 141 of January 1953, Paul Nitze points out that Soviet nuclear capacities are an extremely grave threat to the U.S., and then he gives two reasons. One is that they might inhibit us in carrying out a first strike against the U.S.S.R. The second is that "they would tend to impose greater caution in our cold war policies to the extent that these policies involve significant risks of general war." Now that's a rather pithy comment. It's correct. If the Soviet Union has strategic nuclear forces, that might impose caution on us in our cold war policies. What are they? Intervention and aggression against enemies inside our own domain, and we want to be able to proceed without caution. We'd be afraid that if we attacked somebody, the U.S.S.R. might do something about

it and that would lead to a nuclear war. Nitze was outlining what nowadays is called in the peace movement "the deadly connection," the concern that a Third World conflict might engage the superpowers and lead to nuclear war. We must be able to attack indigenous groups in our own domain in defense of "our" resources without impediment. And note that these cold war policies are not directed against the Russians, but rather against people in our own domains.

The Real Meaning of Deterrence

This is the real meaning of deterrence. Secretary of Defense Harold Brown (under Carter), in his last testimony to Congress in 1980, explained that our strategic nuclear forces provide the framework within which our conventional forces "become meaningful instruments of military and political power." We have indeed been able to use our conventional forces against enemies throughout our domains— South Vietnamese, Filipinos, and so on. This gives us the first real reason (having dispensed with all the fraudulent reasons about "security") for the development of the strategic weapons systems. It's a reason that grows out of deep concerns with world control, with the nature of power in the U.S., with maintaining dominance over others and over the world's wealth.

There's a second major reason for the strategic weapons buildup. Every modern capitalist economy is really state capitalism—the state has to play a major role in organizing the economy. This has been obvious since the Second World War got us out of the Great Depression of the 1930s. If the government subsidizes production in the advanced sectors of industry, a capitalist economy can pull itself out of a depression and keep moving. That lesson, sometimes called "Keynesianism," was learned by everyone, whether they had read Keynes or hadn't. The Fascist powers learned it, we learned it, and nobody's forgotten it. There's one very tempting way for governments to do it—and that's through military spending. This has become our industrial policy. The state creates a guaranteed market for high technology production. Occasionally you'll read ludicrous justifications for this— there was one in the *New York Times* by Malcolm Brown where he points out that nuclear weapons are great because they even contributed to the development of smoke detectors. But the real point is that when the country drifts into recession, the government has to intervene to "get the country moving again" (as Kennedy put it), or to "reindustrialize" (the way Reagan put it). Reagan is called a conservative, but he's probably the most extreme Keynesian in American history. The ratio of government spending to Gross National Product increased more rapidly under Reagan than under any government since the Second World War.

Why do we have to use the military system for this? Any economics department will point out that you could do it in all sorts of other ways. But these technical answers are not pertinent, because they ignore the crucial condition of state policy: it must benefit privileged elites! In 1949, there was a discussion in *Business Week* that concluded that there wouldn't be any great problem in adapting the economy to a peacetime world. But, it explained, from the point of view of the businessman, a military order from the government is basically a gift, a subsidy, the best possible thing. It doesn't interfere with the businessman's prerogatives, his decision-making capacity. It means you can produce any kind of garbage and we'll buy it and furthermore we'll destroy it. Now that's important, because that means he can produce more and we'll destroy that too. That's what a military order is: it is the production of high-technology waste which is subsidized. However, as the article points out, if the President is not able to resort to this device, he's going to have to turn to some other mode of state intervention in the economy, and that's going to lead to welfare state measures, to social programs of all sorts. And that's no good. It's going to have redistributive effects, it's going to organize other constituencies, it's going to change the institutions to the detriment of business. Therefore, obviously, we can't have this—so let's have military spending.

Subsidizing Lethal Waste

Now, you somehow have to get taxpayers to be willing to pay, and the best way of doing that is to frighten them. You can always frighten them because the "monolithic and ruthless conspiracy" is out there ready to take over the world. It's pretty hard to think of a better way to frighten the taxpayer into subsidizing high technology waste.

Those are two solid reasons why the arms race continues, and they are, I think, the real reasons. One, the domestic need to maintain a subsidy for the advanced sectors of the economy; and two, the need to provide an umbrella under which we can act without caution in our cold war policies. From such considerations you can see quite clearly why it doesn't make any difference what public opinion is. You could have 99% of the population supporting a nuclear freeze, and it still wouldn't enter the political system because there are serious issues at stake. There's the question of dominating and controlling the world. There's the question of robbing resources. There's the problem of insuring that domestic power is enhanced, that those who have power in American society get that power strengthened. Now, they are the ones who own and run the society and also run the political system largely, so obviously they're not going to say, "Let's have a nuclear freeze," which is going to change all this radically. So it's just not going to happen.

Telling people to vote for a nuclear freeze and then everything will be wonderful—that's misleading them. You can come out and say you're in favor of a nuclear freeze, but nothing's going to happen because there are serious issues at stake and you'd better understand those issues. If you want the world to survive, you are going to have to face those issues. Just signing a petition isn't going to have any effect.

That ought to be learned, and it will be interesting to see if it is going to be learned. The people who organized the nuclear freeze did succeed in their terms; they got a huge proportion of the population to support it. It was supposed to work because we have a pluralistic democracy. Well, it didn't work; so we have to ask why. Some people have drawn an answer already, and it's a very odd answer: it didn't work because, although we convinced the population, we didn't convince the experts. Well, that's a certain way to make sure the arms race goes on, because the debate among the experts can have only one outcome: let's keep building—because we really can't know if our strategies are going to work or not. That's like saying, "Okay, great, let's have more and more missiles, let's have Star Wars, let's have the next crazy thing they think of, let's have whatever is needed to proceed with our cold war policies and to keep the economy functioning." That's the wrong answer. There are other answers, and they're not easy ones to face, but they're there.

Let me point out that, apart from the waste of resources and the likelihood of destruction, the actual consequences of all this have been pretty grim. There's a study for the Institute of World Order by Ruth Sivard, an arms control expert, that estimates the costs roughly. She counts 125 military interventions, 95% of them in the Third World, 79% of them initiated by the West (meaning essentially the U.S.), 6% initiated by the Communist powers. Well, you know, you can play around with the numbers and maybe challenge this or that, but qualitatively it's right. The human consequences have been incredible. Take just Indochina alone. During the first phase of the war when we were supporting France, about half a million Vietnamese died. From 1954-1965, while the U.S. was engaged in massive terror against South Vietnam, over 160,000 were killed. From 1965-1975, the outright land invasion and expansion of the war, the estimates are that perhaps as many as 3,000,000 Vietnamese, Laotians and Cambodians may have died. That's about 4,000,000 in that decade, considerably more over the whole period.

A Real Victory

That's a lot of people dead. Incidentally, that led to an American victory. It's called an American defeat, but it's really impossible for a country with the power of the U.S. to be defeated by such an adversary. And we weren't. There isn't going to be any social and economic development in Vietnam for at least a century. The country was destroyed and we're keeping maximal pressure on it. At the same time we have built up our support in the surrounding regions to insure that the rot wouldn't spread. For example, in 1965, the U.S. backed a military coup in Indonesia which led to the massacre of about 700,000 people in four months, and that was "great." It was

lauded by American liberals as a wonderful development and given as an argument for the war in Vietnam, which in fact it was.

I won't review the rest of the world—Latin America and elsewhere—but the costs have really been enormous. One part of the cost is the constant threat of nuclear war. In the last twenty years, that threat has existed in the Middle East, where we've come very close to nuclear war. There, the U.S. has been the primary factor preventing a political settlement, maintaining a situation of military confrontation with a strong likelihood of nuclear war. The Pentagon recognizes this. An Air Force study leaked about a year and a half ago, called "Air Force 2000," pointed out that without settlement of the Arab-Israeli Conflict, global war is virtually inevitable; and we are blocking the kind of political settlement that has in fact been feasible for at least a decade.

These comments can be generalized to the U.S.S.R. No doubt each of the superpowers would be delighted to see the other one disappear from the face of the earth. However, long ago each recognized that this is unfeasible. Both superpowers understand that the other can be eliminated only through mutual annihilation, so what has happened actually is that they've settled into a system of accommodation, a system of interaction that is a joint policy of global management. Each creates a nuclear umbrella deterrent system to allow it to carry out without caution its own cold war policies, and those policies are directed against its own satellite countries. For the Russians that means Eastern Europe and now Afghanistan, and for us it means most of the rest of the world. It is a highly functional system in that each of the superpowers is able to mobilize its own population in support of brutal and costly actions within its own domains.

Change the Structures

It's not at all easy to see how we can extricate ourselves, as long as we have fanatics around like Kennedy and Reagan and others whom people pay attention to. Until major institutional changes take place, what we're doing (anybody who's trying to oppose destruction and war) is engaging in a kind of holding action to try to avert catastrophe. It's a little bit like putting a band-aid on a cancer, but that's about the best you can do as long as institutions remain as they are.

There is a kind of short-term rationality to the system, but it's obvious that in the long run it's suicidal. By far the most imminent of all dangers is in fact the "deadly connection," that is, that a Third World conflict will engage the superpowers and lead to a nuclear war. It's not true that all problems in the world result from U.S. initiatives, but we have quite the major share. That is a rather hopeful fact, I think. This means that there's a great deal we can do about it, of course on the condition that we can muster the courage and integrity to face the facts honestly, and then proceed to act in some fashion to change the structures that are causing all of this.

From a speech broadcast by KPFA/FM Pacifica radio in Berkeley, California.

Ivan Argüelles

H-BOMB

speech of false metal in the mineral space
there is no transition we open our eyes
birds' wings beating in the darkness behind the ruins
fear of sheets of open places of broken glass falling
an end to the sequence of wounds received daily
an end to the children's games in the burning circle
dread with its sealed eyelids dread with its compact tooth
they assign dates to its trial and error
the judgement seals the shoes the hotel goes up
in smoke there is no transition just the blank
consuming amnesia the speechless fables about fire
the pallid sun turning from white to black to ash
falling in a rain of shredded paper which fills the hour
the empty moment in the center of all water
behind the corruption of shadow assembled in the bag
the dripping in the eaves the footsteps on the stair
the body in the snow the face behind the ice
the hands inside the mirror the hair in the drawer
symbology of fear treading the rope of air
there is no transition the pages are wild and empty
and knocking at the hidden door the Pirate
with his message of shipwreck and drowning
announces there is no transition not this time
nor any other time the hour fills with what we see
as we proceed directionless through the center of water
deluged with memories of sepulchral beings and truths
the sky bangs open the clouds ring with false metal
we shut our eyes again the hotel collapses silently

Adam Cornford

THE RAPTURE

Perfection is terrible, it cannot have children
—Sylvia Plath

And it came to pass just as they had foretold
the heavy-necked prophets beating the air with the Word
in front of the cameras / quoting chapter and verse
like prices zigzagging up on their futures market
Just as they had foretold / just as they had hoped
the war-boils sputtering in their crusts of bombed-out cities
here and there across the spread-eagled starving earth
burst inward into the major vessels
The poison messages were slammed up toward the heart
slammed down into the tiniest peripheral hut-clusters

And just as the prophets had foretold and pushed for
the overfed power-soaked flesh wired into the gaps
in the circuitry on both sides
followed its own programming
and the silos opened like glittering fircones underground
and the smoke-saplings sprouted out of the landscape
on both sides as the missiles got their chance at last

And just as the prophets had wanted but not entirely believed
in the moment when blindness and deafness detonated
overwhelmingly overhead
the few million True Believers flicked up all at once
out of their shining kitchens / their sparkling cars
their dazzling glass-sided churches
and were sucked / a brief reverse rainshower of bodies
into the now dissolving sky

And just as they had foretold / just as they had smirked about
half the others in their billions were expunged in the first instant
fumed away like damp-spurts under the featureless
glittering press of an iron
and the remaining billions soon after

the swarms of ragged stick-figures in outlying areas
and strategically unimportant countries
came scrabbling to a halt among the rubble / shrivelled
by ash-blizzards and toxin-showers
obliterated in the immeasurable dark fist of frost
All the Damned were forgotten forever
along with ragas conga solos and concertos
and the mad king carrying his daughter in his arms
forgotten along with the tiger's flame-banners
and the gorilla's green meditations
the high-speed skywriting of swallows
and the great equation-chants of the whales

And just as the prophets had foretold / just
as they had staked everything on
the Believers were born again for the third time
waking already modestly dressed in wrinkle-free white
set down in an immense perfected suburb
under a seamless blue astrodome sky
and their triumphant prayers hummed up
like dew in the morning from the immaculate family homes
for the Promise had been fulfilled

Only gradually they began to catch on
as the sun never shifted from the top of perfect noon
the trim lawns stayed trim and never needed weeding
the neatly-planted trees never reddened or shed leaves
their own mouths never juiced after a steak or a sugar-cone
the malls of their brains never closed up and darkened for sleep
their children never grew by a millimeter
Everything was made of the same smooth perfection
even their eyeballs
were as dry and slick as nylon bearings
and when some of them tried walking away
they found themselves coming after a few miles
inexplicably back on their tracks

And gradually they began to catch on
that the sun that never moved overhead was not

a sun at all but His vast eye-pupil / a furnace door open
to admit their tiny image into the remorseless brilliance
of His brain / where the ranked angels
slid coruscating up and down like fuel-rods
Out of their terrified cramped longings had come
a local Sky-Father with His own bubble of eternity
and now they were truly in His sight forever
ageless and bloodless and undead
just as their prophets had foretold

Elsewhere / in time
the earth fanned its upper air clear of corpse-dust
it sluiced its corrugations with cycle after cycle of rain
drew cushiony lichens over its burn-scars
dismantled isotopes and aldehydes
With the help of the commonplace changing star
it still orbited / year after year
it began to repair its experiment / its elaborate
squirming mildewed life-carpet
As the gene-ladders went on dividing into mistake after mistake
patiently the earth went on sorting these possibilities
with its probes of heat and cold / its delicate
scalpels of predation
It set out to re-invent forests from scrawny chaparral
marlin and sunfish from a glimmer of sprats
deer-jump / owl-glide / lemur-swing
from a few furry chitterings hidden away in burrows

Meanwhile the countless energy-shards
of its former inhabitants / the Damned
drifted slowly out among the lights of the galaxy
like the invisible tang of smoke from a hanging lantern
puffed out and lit again
in one corner of a city where the festival goes on

Marie Wilson, *The Triumph of Order Over Chaos*

from

The First and the Last: A Woman Thinks about War

SUSAN GRIFFIN

The story of atomic warfare began in silence. While scientists designed a nameless weapon and a battalion of men trained for an unknown mission, a whole city was built in Tennessee whose purpose was hidden.

Is it possible that a mind can break from the weight of what is known and yet unknown? Those who worked in the factories at Oakridge were not told that they were making the fissionable material to be used in atomic weapons. Almost none of the military men assigned to this project knew its purpose. But, however a secret is kept, it will make its way, like an object lighter than water and meant to float, to the surface. A Navy ensign posted to Oakridge suffers a mental breakdown. Is he the repository for the unspoken fears of others? He begins to rave about a terrible weapon that will soon bring about the end of the world. Because his ravings are close to the truth, the Navy builds a special wing of the hospital at Oakridge for him, staffed with psychiatrists, physicians, orderlies and janitors, each chosen especially for this work, judged trustworthy, and able to keep secrets. The ensign is given continual sedation. Whenever he begins to speak, he receives another injection. His family is told that he is on a long mission at sea.

How strange it is that some lives become emblematic of our times. What is it that makes us recognize madness in another? I imagine the speech of this man. He utters only fragments, broken phrases, that do not make sense. Perhaps he repeats the word *terrible* over and over, punctuating his speech only occasionally with the word *weapon* or *death*. Perhaps he uses the phrase *end of the world* but surrounded in a labyrinth of personal associations, a childhood name for a brother, a fearful memory from a nightmare, a word known only to him but meant as a key to unlock his private suffering, the experience that sometime in his past broke him. Not only what he says, but also his broken mind evokes a story that is true— neutrons released from atoms fracture other atoms until the circumference does not hold and there is one vast breaking.

Oakridge was a closed city. Its occupants had to carry badges of identification. They would enter and leave through an armed guard house. Regular buses would take wives into Knoxville so that they could carry back the small necessities of life—groceries, a pair of socks, electric light bulbs. Otherwise what they needed was provided for them inside the city walls— schools, churches, movies, dances. The gates stayed closed for three years after the war. When they were opened a parade was arranged down the main street. Marie "the body" MacDonald rode in an open car through the gates. She was followed by a brass band. And speeches. At Elza gate a circle of children cowered into the arms of their parents as they watched a magnesium flare produce a miniature mushroom cloud.

A photograph of this occasion was published in a book celebrating the twenty-fifth anniversary of Oakridge. I was given this book by a woman I met in Oakridge last winter. I sat in her living room with her and her daughter Angeline as she told me the story of her life. I will call her Edna.

She was born in North Carolina, in 1914. Her father was a sample weaver. He had no formal education but he was always reading. The range of his interest was wide. Physics. The forgotten books of the Bible. Edna always wanted to know where it was that he had gone as a young man.

My father had little education, and he spoke in the grammar of working men, but he had the same hunger to know, a curiosity and an openness. We would speak of many subjects together, arguing dispassionately, never with rancor. He often agreed with my perceptions which gave me a confidence rare in a girl.

Edna took after her father, reading and thinking. And her brother, Jack, who was like him too. Edna's father adored this son. In 1941, against his father's wishes, Jack enlisted. Later that year, after the Japanese attack on Pearl Harbor, America entered the war. When he heard the news of this attack, Edna's father had a stroke. And that Christmas Eve, he died. Edna believed her father chose to die so he would not have to suffer the death of his own son. Jack died on D-Day in Normandy. The young man who came to tell Edna's mother of this death could say nothing. He just sat and cried, as did Edna when she told me of these two deaths. I had asked her what she thought when she learned of the atomic bomb. "I didn't think," she said, "I was just glad the war was over."

Edna met her husband before this war, when she was just sixteen. She was already graduated from high school and had gone to work in the hosiery mill. She made the seams of the stockings that eventually were carried by soldiers going overseas. She married at seventeen. Her husband worked in the cotton mill. Bill drank and one night he got into serious trouble. By then they had two children and one more on the way. He said he was forced to do what he did by the two men who gave him a lift. She never knew whether or not he was telling her the truth. The charge was serious because a gun was used. But he was young, so he was sent to reform school, and that was where he learned to be a machinist.

Jobs were hard to find. And then he was offered a job with very good pay. The management paid for the whole family to visit Oakridge. They were put up in a hotel and a limousine came to drive them to the plant. Edna understood almost nothing of what she saw as they passed through the plant. Over the years, her husband told her little. She picked up a bit of information here and there. That uranium is a soft metal when it is machined. That the doctors found high levels of mercury in his blood. He had dropped a beaker of it, and had been tracking it home on the bottoms of his shoes. It was on the carpet where the children played.

He was told to keep the work he did a secret from everyone, even his family. He himself did not know the whole truth, and he accepted this. But his mind worked all the time, even so. He was an intelligent man. He had constructed a valve essential for the manufacture of uranium into fissionable material. He never knew what the valve was for but he pieced together an idea from incidents and rumors. A boy shut out by his father's silence learns not to ask questions but to find his answers in other ways. One day a man dropped a block of ice while he was delivering it. It fell with a loud crashing sound and the scientists he worked with panicked, running in all directions. From what he gathered to be the truth, he made his own deci-sion. He moved his wife Edna and their children back to Carolina until the war was over. He did not tell her why.

After the war, Edna's husband returned briefly to Carolina, but he could find no work. Edna stopped working in the mills after her fourth child. The family moved back to Oak-ridge. Now, six of her ten children work there, some as scientists and engineers, tutored by their mother's love of knowledge. Edna's husband is retired now with a lung disease the plant doctors tell him came from smoking. She and her husband lead separate lives, rarely speaking, except for practical reasons.

I was born in 1943, the year Edna came to Oakridge. My mother and father were troubled in their marriage and I was conceived to hold them together. In marrying my mother my father drew into his life all the hidden sorrows of his childhood and made for me the same circumstances he had suffered. Long before I was born my mother began to have a problem with drinking. This problem grew worse. We shared a house with my mother's parents.

For years I lived with my grand-mother. My father would come to visit me on weekends. He was often late. And I was often waiting for him. Since his death I have had many dreams in which he returns to me. He comes with many faces, but he is always dead. When he died I had the feeling that he had never really lived, and left the earth, unfinished. We spent many hours together and had many conversations but never once did he speak to me of the pain that I could see at times in his eyes. He had a loneliness as of a man in solitary confinement who still walks among others. Was he a vague presence even to himself, a fragment leaving only traces on the face of this earth, trailing unclaimed ghosts?

One of his ghosts inhabits me. In our hours together I breathed in the irresolution of his unspoken feelings. Like my father, I have committed small suicides daily. Not going to the heart of all I feel, I have erased my real presence, sexuality, intelligence from language and expression.

Perhaps it was because there was so much unspoken between my father and me that we loved to go to the movies. We would go to Grauman's Chinese theater where the stars had molded their hands into unsettled concrete. I would fit my smaller hand into these depressions. And then go with my father into the dark theater, where we waited to see the screen light up with color, motion, and momentous feeling.

To say one of their names was to evoke a world of feeling. We watched them all. Alan Ladd. Katherine Hepburn. Cary Grant. Brilliant and luminous. They were our icons. Rita Hayworth. The love goddess. She posed for this photograph on a prop bed, wearing a negligee from the wardrobe department. From birth she was groomed to be a film star.

She was as much shaped by her father as I was by mine. Eduardo Cansino was a professional dancer. He taught his daughter Marguerita all that he knew. Then, at the age of thirteen, she began to dance as his partner. No one in the audience knew she was a child. She was dressed seductively. On stage they performed a romantic duet, dancing in lock-step, ending faces in profile, kissing. Off stage, Eduardo locked her in her dressing room, while he would go to drink and gamble. For years, he managed her career, introducing her to men who made films. Then, she married a man her father's age, who did all that her father had done before.

I remember the night my father discovered I had made love with a boy. I never saw him so angry with me. He shouted at me. Slapped me. Then, when he tucked me into bed, he put his lips over my ear and blew softly. Who was I to him at this moment? This was the only sexual gesture he ever made toward me. But still, we did our own lock-step. I have been his partner in despair.

When I was only two years old, Rita Hayworth made a famous film called *The Lady From Shanghai*. It was directed by Orson Welles, who was then her husband. He played the hero, and she the heroine. The hero, a detective in "the most wicked city in the world," is drawn by the heroine's beauty into danger. Slowly she entraps him. They enter a house of mirrors. She points her gun outward at him and at us who watch as the story concludes. The gun explodes and the mirror is shattered. But, the hero lives. It is the evil lady who dies. Of course, we too survive.

It was in 1945, in the January of that year, that I became two years old, and in the same year, in August, two atomic bombs were dropped over Japan, in Hiroshima and then Nagasaki. I remember a faded bookmark from this time. I found it in my grandmother's books. A caricature of a Japanese man, painted yellow, glowers over a lit match. Behind him a small green forest bursts into flame.

Is it possible that Helen of Troy was only a caricature of a woman? In one version of that story it is said that she was never really in Troy at all, and that what the Greek armies saw was only a phantom. The blast at Hiroshima left phantoms of a kind, shadows instantly impressed by object, parts of buildings, fleeing people who existed one moment and then in the fraction of a second vanished into vapor.

Last fall, when I traveled to Hiroshima, I asked to meet a woman my age, who, like me, would have been two years old when the bomb exploded. Sumiko Yamada was thrown through the air and out a window, on August 5, 1945. She still has two small scars on her face where the glass was embedded. But she does not remember the blast.

Her father had disappeared in the explosion. They had searched for his bones or his ashes but no sign of him could be found. His passage from life could not be consecrated. Her mother, very badly burned, lived until August 23, when she died of radiation sickness. The two small children were left alone. They were taken in by relatives; but, her loneliness did not end. She

moved in rotation between five different houses. An extra child was a burden. She carried her belongings in a scarf and opened them in a corner of a room. She had no room or bed of her own. Many times she sat and listened as her relatives argued over who should take her next. Somewhere inside herself, she felt she had no reason to exist. She was like a neutron, lost from its path of meaning, without a matrix, with no world of relation. She went to her middle school by a train that passed over a bridge. And while the train would make its way over this bridge, she thought of taking her own life.

I nodded as she told me this story and I told her mine. How I too, the child of a different kind of divorce, was moved from house to house. Between us a kind of knowledge passed, half spoken, half unspoken. We both understood that what we felt had come from circumstances and not from a flaw in ourselves.

Such a childhood settles into flesh and bone. It can be seen. It is not invisible but present in the line of shoulders, the measure of breath, a hand moving to lips, so that even a story not told is told over and over again in mimed gestures of shyness and fear and conscribes a place in the body holding this old suffering almost with tenderness. Sumiko has not spoken of her childhood to her husband, not to her children.

How much do we know or not know in those we love? Love is, in some way, a kind of seeing, through which many intricate facts are embraced. What is hidden, kept secret, cannot be loved. It exists in a place of exile, outside the realms of response.

In a famous short story about the bombing of Hiroshima, a man who is poisoned with radiation returns home to his village. He tells his family and friends what he has seen. No one believes him until news reports arrive. Then, they listen to his story with shock and grief. But after a time, they no longer want to hear his story. He is condemned to repeat what he has witnessed over and over to those who do not listen.

Some argued that because of the high intelligence of the people of Kyoto, this city would be the best target for the first atomic bomb. These citizens, it was said, would best be able to appreciate the significance of the new weapon. But Kyoto was not chosen. Secretary of State Stimpson felt the city too beautiful to be destroyed. Kyoto has for many centuries been the home for an ancient and gracious cul-

ture. Its streets are resplendent with temples, gardens; it is the center for the manufacture of silk and the practice of the tea ceremony.

Beauty lies at the heart of the tea ceremony. Each object used must be beautiful. Special cups are made for this ceremony. Even to look on these cups is to be brought into a wider, calmer realm of the self. The tea master Okakura Kukuzo has said that beauty evokes harmony and the mystery of mutual charity. What became at one point in history an art reserved for the Samurai warrior is really the distillation of all the ways that women had of shaping life. Ways of setting a table, design in fabric, old recipes, songs, ways of bowing, of serving, of sitting. All that we call beautiful, the shape of a balcony, a certain landscape, a phrase, an alphabet, the curve of an airplane wing, a mathematical formula, is a kind of vessel, like love, that holds what we know.

Marie Wilson, *Sun Power*

Hokusai's *Manga*

ROBERT GLÜCK

A samurai tracks through woods watched by the supernatural, which he knows (tiles of
carp scale, coromorant feathers for thatch) *but momentarily forgets.*
Struggle between ancient houses, ridicule, confusion:

A warrior bragged about his strength; finally he was summoned to a wrestling
tournament. He rode through a maple forest of "burning leaves" where he caught
a glimpse of an attractive woman dressed in indigo cloth and carrying a bucket
of water on her head. The woman was thinking about clumsiness, about a maid-
servant who dropped one of a set of ten treasured porcelain bowls decorated
with long-haired turtles in gold and silver lusters. The master berated her so
severely that she jumped into an old well where, from that night, you could hear
her hollow voice counting and recounting the remaining dishes. The warrior
dismounted and caught the woman's hand. The woman didn't resist but said
dreamily, eyes on the distance, "—or if it rains from a low cloud, or if a shadow
half covers a valley, or a lagoon, or if it doesn't, or if a tree branch looks
particularly attractive in itself, surely not because it resembles an elephant's gray
leg—"

The warrior sees this as encouragement. He gently takes her arm and the
woman releases her hold on the bucket and clamps his wrist under her armpit
with such force that a line of cranes whizzes past the couple and nature divides
in front of them and rejoins behind. The warrior tries to escape; he digs in his
heels and ripples his muscles but he can't pull free, and the woman marches
serenely on. The warrior isn't the first who fell in love with a dead person or
who misjudges the power of his beloved—or that death should be the basis of
her strength. No wonder he's outclassed. We can have no idea of how many
ghosts there are or how many people love them; they seem irresistible to a
certain type who hungers for excellence.

She's thinking about revenge, about a
cousin who was born ugly because her mother drowned the cousin's half-sister
by an earlier marriage. The cousin inherited an acre by the river, so a peasant

married and then murdered her. For years she haunted the riverside, driving the peasant's subsequent wives to their deaths.

Now the warrior pleads to be set free, says he's due at a wrestling match. The woman laughs. "I have a little story to tell you. A giant said, 'Nothing can fell me.' A hero replied, 'A little thing can fell you.' The hero dashed forward and drove a pick through the giant's little toe. The giant roared, transmuted pain into rage and scooped up the hero who said, 'Now I'm going to rent a room at the corner of Hell Street and I shall be happy to see you whenever you pass by.' The giant tore him in half the long way and threw both pieces up so high they disappeared. It was a stunning victory for giants and monsters."

Earlier, the warrior felt he had mastered the subject of death. Soon she will teach him that once you master a subject the subject masters you. Later the warrior will locate under every smell the sweet pointed decadence, even though the leaves are on their trees. Now they embark on a relationship in which every intimacy is rejected; her bucket will not even spill a drop. The warrior still doesn't know she's a ghost; if he could glance down he would see that she has no feet. "You! Wrestling! Live with me for three weeks—I'll toughen you up!"

Philip Lamantia

DIANA GREEN

Of that spider weaving reality I can't speak
to pink it up under paper
riding away on invisible webs stopped by specular turns
These tiny living things happen to the King in his Bath
digression to a strange unhealthy place the first seen Great-tailed Grackle
    signifies mandibles true north Devi-Deva

               'Could he be serious about all those esoteric ideas?'
that resolves everything into dust whose remains are alkaline salt
Go read it with supernatural teeth muttering a winged language
What if it were the moment before the perfect whole?

Watching months of decadence go by
Pluto retrograde five degrees into Scorpio 'It's nothing, just an appearance'
    Several hundred million humans
billions of birds
would have fried inst. if a second space shuttle had been launched after the first
    auto-destructed
What is shows up   galloping the inner image   the finest mirror to the
    absolute clock across a sunlit room Never forget it as you come over the
    horizon, *Hu-mun-u* (sounds like human, an approximate of *Ornithos*)
before it seems to gush to the buttercup wild thistles reeds and fruity trees where
    once there was only Crissy Field*
             From the femur bones of language there'll be nineteen varieties

---

*Crissy Field, a semiwild, relatively barren strip of land fronting Frisco Bay, frequented by birders and joggers. There, I saw in Spring 1986 a U.S. Army tractor driving over the nesting territory of Kildeer birds (theoretically protected by the Dept. of the Interior), crushing eggs and turning helpless fledglings into corpses.

of Oak to meet you any day of the week 'The skeleton of solitude' once writ is
      writ again
and the temple of Luxor goes over it in a transparency to catch it before it goes
      A Vision of Synarchic Bioregions over Northern California's haunted scapes
            Redwood powers in those fires across the Bay
up river to Mount Shasta
                        and below the Oregon Caves
I've become this sublimating hand attuned to a darkness of sudden light on
      simulacra: the Great Green Faery Head thrust from redwood roots in the
      Humboldt Woods
            luminist sheen
we were Devi-Deva sure
with the wrap of words penetrating wood
I like the old legend: this paper writes me working from predetermined
      feathers
            a mancy of chance
                  delivered by Necessity
                        from the Mistress of the Birds
When we knew her under giant ferns Madumba's world from an ocean of her
      crystal palace
This calls for an Ode a Dawn Feast
Red-faced Cormorant will be there Magnificent Frigate Bird and the Red-
      Crowned of all species This imaginary avefauna suggests more terror before
      ritual indents a world indeed
meditated from a bow string
to speak a visible language
when you began   where you'll end   to begin again   Preserving fire
What moves the aging man closing a car door going slowly up to a metal gate
      The alchemic lesson after seeing what 'Steal fire' means Geometry is that key
                  older than Paleolithic
                  Attar's birds to the sun
I lean to that philosophic fire in caves   seashells   in the slow stalagmatic of
      geologic light
                  Surface only is ours to see below Reason
                              reflect the Black Sun

            Every autumn Nature has a way of showing that dragon-knot of
      iridescent rot
Any forest sends up a message
            clear   non-occulted   lux of darkness
                  green ogre of putrefactional life Poets are speleologists at best

to see on rocks off shore The Language of the Birds

The clear-obscure of symbolical tropes
    zings cosmic pleasures of laryngeal thought

Become my own cave? No easy matter   There's a reversal of those actions
    which may turn into gestures 'These things I'm talkin' about'
Why not dare the despised? No sooner done than asked

Precious stones dance in a ring to distinguish a redpoll's song from the local
    finches
                (see to it, mercurial eminence, resolve it by contraries)
Fierce wild beings presage our transformation into salt — the whole past burnt
    into a phoenix nest — and leave a way open even if the
    smallest   whatever great took off long ago

        Flash back
to tinted windows at the Canteen Dances
The couples were chummy and smelly going to war ordinary rainy night Frisco
    cooked up just before nightfall Ovens flew open beneath their tasty uniforms
    Years later Nuclear Boat in the Harbor Sam Spade comes over Archer downing
    Mickey Mouse and Donald Duck

        The horizon's turned over to read the *medu-Neter*
        The great crystal pool Starry Night breaks into caves
        There's such a sky   instant colorations   green to magenta
            harmonic doubles of ascending letters
                dropped with leaf life
to the fogs of midsummer Doors expressionists slam An attempt to photoreal
    insomnia
There's no closure, sweetbrier Heightened teeth   for the vowel's intent from
    whence it situates
transmutable power

        a hand too languorous for drawing

this palm of oneiromancy can be read for thought, *if thought*, is diamond dust
'In harmless radioactive fallout'
on the way to the Rainbow Café
between the harmony of Clashing Rocks
there's a marsh and a meadow to call back the beasts

'Your love affair with the birds'

Again the quintessential multicolored wild finches chirp round a tunnel an aerial
    way through the great game
Talking about divine emptiness (idiot-maniacal) I'm interlocking chips from
    memory's arcane shift to it
        Mirror-specks devolve
to the Labyrinth Sacrifice seems sempiternal There's something about the
    ecstatic virgins of sacrifice that ties into our Subject when finches land swiftly
to fold out synesthetical displays at the brink of the world That tribelet's
    misnomer, 'Ohlone'
        mystery of holding a banner a stream of that next corner around
a trail into redwood bark to imagine
bubbling beer of manzanita berries when Coyote made love to thousands of
    Dianas

Proportional to the salt of the myth
Orpheus has the ticket from Daladano to the unique Fern Forest fronting Violent
    Ocean

        Spirit of transfigured space
        perfect equipoise
from having traveled to find and to have found it Poor Medium
There's hard-headed search for it among pebbles
radishes of crooked streets
marbles with knickers a naturalist in English woods of the 1920s
        between vectors but dreaming
and isn't it with daydreams that poetry begins to dance?

        Over Land's End touch Terra with your toes

        Someday to hear poetry from a cave
as the poetry of caves ignites all centers of Gaea's embers of new light
Given that flutter of sparrow wings to the tree
        Isis
        Diana
other nameless names
crossing over dimly with my portmanteau Down channel
the way so fogged meeting all that which opposes itself *Coagula* at Crystal Lake
    Imaginary devi spin rock castles of green shadows and the flaming dragon
    completes a torment *That was you, ISIS*

sounds of gentle birds through them
luminous night that fades

a simplistic symbol from the invisible forest
signifies in emerald stone
the difficult restoration of the word
primal principle of Affinity

in Diana's glass   the birds

The Language of Birds

PHILIP DAUGHTRY

"When the trees were enchanted
there was hope for the trees"
—Cad Goddeu

In Northumberland where I was a country lad, birds were viewed as magical allies. Because the birds are free they were said to move in harmony with a flow of earthly energies. The reality of our battered Celtic desire was to hold onto nature as a resource of vision and of power. Power, in the ordinary landed sense of knowing the power of place was our will-spirit; important to coalminers, shipbuilders, farmers and fisherfolk who seldom owned land to work or to hunt and who had been molded into "working-class" peasants by a caste system that internalized integrity generally.

My own grandfather was a regimental sergeant major, retired; a soft-spoken fury of a man who kept pigeons. His birds were homing pigeons and frequently tested against the expanse of the North Sea. The myth of a carrier pigeon flung back to their use in battle long ago when such birds shuttled messages among the tribes. In battle, as in hunting, magic was not to be neglected. The art of breeding and flying birds had a circling lore to its every phase. Grandfather spent hours with his birds, divining their quality, mixing their food with many shrugged-off secrets about his ingredients.

Explanations for the excellence of a bird's flight were woven into the bones of a man's luck. "Luck" as Loki has it ... is the work of an illuminated will, plain magic cast from spirit. Luck and Fate (wyrd) combined with Craft to form the three elements necessary to control a wheeling bird, necessary to strike a soul from afar, necessary to any work of love, warfare or gardening ... deeds of the Great Strand which meant anything done with intention.

Such labor extended to sheepdogs, to horses and to survival. My grandfather spent four years in France during World War II without a scratch. When I walked in the village with him, men and women fell aside, he never paid for a drink, his wyrd was a glowing thing.

Certainly grandfather's birds flew home and stood as sleek golden-eyed queens or hurled their cuckolding chests around the ducket. On rare occasion a peregrine bird would assault the flight but this event was an obvious challenge by nature, a force that chose the weakest or the best of the best with equanimity and ate them ... a Celtic tradition, sacrifice.

Watching a flight hurl itself around the smoking stacks of our village was an exercise in winnowing, all things were winnowed, birds too were part of the worldly game of scrabble, and if things went poorly, there was always rum.

But pigeons were the homefront of birdlore. ("Bird" is a Northumbrian word. Anglo Saxon for bird is "beord" ... although in Geordie ... my native dialect ... we say "board," mixed as we are with the whole shift of vowels: aa div'n knaa.

In fields and estates of a seldom seen nobility, there were other birds to reckon: partridge, pheasant, curlew, kestrels, lapwings, plovers, coots, grebes, snipe, swans, and cuckoos among a hedgerow host of larks, finches, pippits, warblers, tits, blackbirds, thrushes, flycatchers, robins, nuthatches and wood doves to name my memory more than the richness of birds in that corner of England. But we studied the birds, and we were keen. In 1952 many of our mob were still sharp from the War and we had kin with wounds and there were bombcraters in the fields and a working life flavored with a modern desperateness. It seemed a healing to run and map our land and speak openly of what was there. Sure, some farmers raised fists at us, waved shotguns or sent ass-ripping terriers to challenge a mother's or a doctor's sewing, but in our hearts all of the land was ours.

Small things to the wisdom of birds.

Just to hear a cuckoo was a call from the wild side of one's life and an excuse to touch what was ordinarily forbidden. For my wandering squad, a cuckoo's call meant it was time to reckon the season, raid apple, cherry or pear orchards, or simply lurk around a girl scout camp and watch the lasses' shadows as they undressed in their tents at night, or we'd rise to some unsettled argument and settle it with blood or "run cuckoo"—spontaneously daft, leaving zigzag tracks in the oats, a sure invitation to the dogs. If a farmer tracked us home it meant the police. Cuckoos were a problem ... aye.

But we dare not stone a cuckoo although we took them as temporary pets, fascinated at their greed. We'd take an egg from a meadow pippit if it was alone in the nest and twice as large as it should be, but squabbles always arose as to whether it was a cuckoo's egg or not. Cuckoos imitated the eggs of their hosts spontaneously, we believed; a cuckoo could copycat, that was for certain. The bloody cuckoo was a wyrd bird ... canny, a bit too mixed in its allegiances to theft and to song. And a lad can't forget a cuckoo's song. A cuckoo's song struck a human like encountering, say, a casual jaguar on a trail to the river in Belize ... seizing the heart with the rush of wilderness.

And with the fierceness of cuckoos we saw our fields as wild: there were rough men and dairy bulls to challenge anytime and the oddball gamekeeper with a weasel face; but these were obvious obstacles and interfered little with our focus, the birds.

We could poach and pluck a partridge after the fashion of a fox, and scatter the feathers near a den. A fox was blameless, we were not. We could snare rabbits and skin them like socks turned inside out, but left that for a great hunger which never came. We could shimmy up a pine trimmed to its knots, a bare trunk to protect nesting hawks. We would peek in that great musky twigdom at the chicks if the hawk's rage allowed us. Hawk eggs were left alone, a hawk was cause for whispering, too much like bank robbery for the lads we were.

We were beaten by swans. A swan's wing was capable of a blow like a Parisian cop's leaded cape, arm-breaking. Swans were all royal birds, enchanting, elegant and big. We'd wade out with handfuls of sedge to offer them. But if we spied eggs on their reed nest our lust hatched its plot ... build a raft, paddle out ... take an egg ... lift them ... see them! But swans are merciless with a rage worse than any teacher's sharp strap. We were meek in our defeat and learned to strike as a swan strikes ... leaving the pair to cruise the wet meadows.

We might see a snipe with a flight like the imagined shape of lightning zigzagging along a hedgerow. We'd run like snipe, slalom around tuffets of marshgrass and clumps of thistle learning the snipecraft of escape with equal delight of a charge. What we learned from the birds was all a flight, of sorts.

Or we'd dismantle a churchwall after a flycatcher's nest hidden deep in the stone; a task that demanded lookouts, tools and longer arms and thinner wrists than were available. We became canny with stone and studied how to replace a stone so it might be lifted to reveal a nest unless, by luck, the wall decided to fall on us.

Or we'd hunt a coastal field after curlew nests and find none although the long-legged, long-billed birds wheeled and haunted us with their ghosting cry. We walked hours with a furious numbing intent in the chill northern air knowing that to quit was a relief to all but to quit was to cast suspicion upon one's repute for other endurances.

Unless, after years, we came home and decided never to hunt eggs, rather to follow the birds and reckon the sighting of rare species as good news. Although it was my quest to find a wren and watch it fashion a nest ... an event my grandfather said needed to be done alone, by stealth, if such a nest might ever be found. A wren was a druid's bird and mysterious, not to say small. I found one, its long stock woven in the dryhair'd branchings of a spidery thicket. I lay there and lie there still, sensing the pattern as it is woven, hearing the song as it pips through my breath, embracing the design that that language taught me.

Keeping True to Earth

EDWARD ABBEY

The Bible says that "the love of money is the root of all evil." But what is the essential meaning of money? Money gives us the means to command the labor and service and finally the very lives of others—human or otherwise. Money means power. I would expand the Biblical aphorism, therefore, in this fashion: the root of all evil is the love of power.

Power attracts the worst and corrupts the best. It is no accident that police work, for example, tends to attract those (if not only those) with the bully's instinct. And put a captain's bars on an ordinary, decent man, give him a measure of arbitrary power over others, and he becomes—unless a man of unusual character—a martinet, another petty despot. Power corrupts; and as Lord Acton pointed out, absolute power corrupts absolutely.

The problem of anarchism is the problem of power—how to keep power decentralized, equally distributed, democratized. Anarchism, in my view, means simply the maximum possible dispersal of power: political power, economic power, and force—military power. An anarchist society would consist of a voluntary association of self-reliant, self-supporting, autonomous communities. An anarchist community would consist (as it did in pre-agricultural, pre-industrial times) of a voluntary association of free and independent families, self-reliant and self-supporting, but bound by friendship, kinship, and a tradition of mutual aid.

Anarchism is democracy taken seriously—as it is in Switzerland today, where issues of national importance are decided by a direct vote of all citizens—and taken all the way, in every major sector of social life. Political democracy will not survive in a society which permits a few to accumulate economic power over the many (e.g., the U.S. today). Nor in a society which delegates police power and military power to an elite corps of professionals. (Sooner or later the professionals will take over.)

In my notion of an anarchistic community every citizen would be armed, trained, and capable when necessary of playing the part of policeman or soldier. A healthy community polices itself; a healthy society would do the same. By the identical principle each would have the will and the means to defend itself against hostile powers from outside. (Assuming an approximate technological parity.)

Anarchy does not mean civil breakdown—total disorder. Why do we call in the National Guard when disaster disrupts a community? Only because, as in a feudal society, we have allowed an overlord—centralized government—to assume powers which we should have retained for ourselves. Looters, thugs, criminals may appear anywhere, anytime, but in nature such types are mutants, anomalies, a minority; the members of a truly democratic (anarchistic) community would not require outside assistance in dealing with them. You may call this vigilante justice: I would call it democratic justice. Better to have all citizens participate in the suppression and punishment of crime—and share in the moral responsibility—than turn the nasty job over to some quasi-criminal type (or hero) in a uniform with a tin badge on his shirt.

Yes, we need heroes. And heroines. But they should serve only as inspiration and examples, never as leaders. Anarchy, let us remember, does not mean "no rule"; it means "no rulers." The distinction is fundamental.

Decentralizing civilization—the basic goal of anarchism—is the exact opposite of advocating a "world order" strong enough to crush any would-be conqueror. Such an entity would itself be an instrument of conquest and would fall, sooner or later, into the hands of the power-lovers. Government is a social machine whose function is coercion through centralized Power—domination. Like a bullldozer, government serves the caprice of any person—philosopher or madman—who succeeds in seizing the levers of control. A world government equipped with supreme power suggests a planetary tyranny. The purpose of anarchism is to dismantle power institutions and to prevent their reconstruction.

Who will govern the governors? Ten thousand years of human history demonstrate that our freedoms cannot be entrusted to those ambitious few who are drawn to power; we must learn—again—to govern ourselves.

Is the USA an example of beneficent government? It is true that life in America at this time is far better, for the majority, than in most (not all) other nations. But that fact does not excuse our failings. Judged by its intentions and potentials, the great American experiment appears to me as a failure. We have not become a nation of independent freeholders, as Jefferson envisioned; nor have we evolved into a true democracy—government by the people—as Lincoln imagined. Instead we see the realization of the scheme devised by Madison and Hamilton: a strong centralized state which promotes and protects the accumulation of private wealth on the part of a few while reducing the majority to the role of dependent employees of state and industry.

We are a nation of helots ruled by an oligarchy of techno-military-industrial administrators. Never before in history have serfs been so well fed, well medicated, craftily flattered and lavishly entertained—but we are serfs nonetheless. Our debased popular culture—TV, rock music, home video, processed food, mechanical recreation—is the culture of slaves.

Furthermore, the whole grandiose structure is self-destructive: by enshrining the profit motive (power) as our guiding ideal, we encourage the intensive and accelerating use and abuse of land, air, water—the natural world—on which the structure depends for its continued existence.

A house built on greed cannot long endure. Whether called capitalism or communism makes little difference; both of these oligarchic, militaristic, expansionist, acquisitive, industrializing and technocratic systems are driven by the greed for power over nature and human nature; both are self-destroying.

Even without the accident of a nuclear war, I predict that the military-industrial state will disappear from the surface of Earth within fifty years. That belief is the basis of my inherent optimism, the source of my hope for the coming restoration of a higher civilization: scattered human populations, modest in number, that live by fishing, hunting, food-gathering, small-scale farming and ranching, that assemble once a year in the ruins of abandoned cities for great festivals of moral, spiritual, artistic and intellectual renewal—a people for whom the wilderness is not a playground but their natural and native home.

New dynasties will arise; new tyrants will appear. But I think that we must and we can resist such recurrent aberrations by keeping loyal to our basic animal nature. Humans were free before the word "freedom" became necessary. Slavery is a cultural invention. Liberty is life: *eros* plus *anarchos* equals *bios*.

Long live anarchy!

13427 Poèmes Metaphysiques
JULIEN BLAINE

13427 POEMES METAPHYSIQUES, POEME N° 220

13427 POEMES METAPHYSIQUES, POEME N° 2

BOUDDHA

13427 POEMES METAPHYSIQUES, POEME NUMERO 67

. Blanche sourit en pensant à la décision qu'elle venait de prendre.

13427 POEMES METAPHYSIQUES, POEME NUMERO 70

OP.CIT.

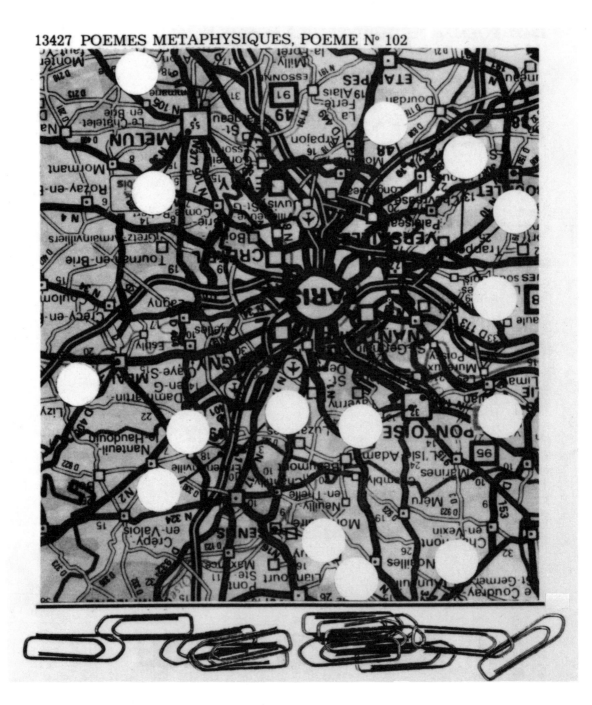

13427 POEMES METAPHYSIQUES, POEME Nº 102

13427 POEMES METAPHYSIQUES POEME N° 13410

EZRA

LIVRE

Marie Ponsot

OUTSIDE THE FERTILE CRESCENT

Too long out of her seashell, too far away
from green waves sparkling as they lick the sky,
Aphrodite falters. Shallow ponds delay
her sea-search. Off course, inland, tired, dry,
she takes a man's words seriously
when he offers water. He owns a well.
She settles in his oasis. His one tree,
his human heart, cast their spell;
for such implosion she serves him gratefully.
He keeps her safe from his city of those
who are wicked. She gets water enough,
cupfuls, pitcherfuls, to cook & wash clothes,
not to plunge in. Pillared when she calls his bluff,
at dawn her salt crystals gleam, flushed with rose.

HARD-SHELL CLAMS

When it was too late for him to provide
his own share in my happy childhood, my
father stopped clowning out stories & tried
for a whole day to see me—a good try
by both of us. Back we went to the seaside
of old summers, we two, we talked, we swam,
sleek with cocoa butter that caught the sand—
a glitter like chain-mail guarding who I am
from his used blue gaze that stared to understand.
Closed, stuck closed, I watched us—far me far him—
go small, smaller, further, father, joy dim
in beach light. Our last chance, last perfect day.

We laughed. We ate four dozen hard-shell clams.
We swallowed what I would not let us say.

ON THE 80th BIRTHDAY
OF A GREAT LADY

She is as she was, a beauty, as expected.
Charm her gun, amor, armour, lifework, birthright,
she looks at men as if she liked the sight.
Gems, fans, allegiances she has collected
keep her contempt secret & undetected;
her self-praise righteous, hard-earned; her glance sure;
her face like an idea of faces, pure;
her hunger private, ill-met, uncorrected.
Her code: "Pretend you are right. Star. Look brave.
As principal player, demand support. Fail
to recall your self. Do sex tricks. Cast your slaves
in revenge plays. Lie. Dock the dog's tail.
Weak? spite weakness. Spite love as weakness. Love spite."

She feels free. 80 years in jail day & night.

Marilyn Hacker

THEN

I was due home at seven, and you were
staying downtown. We shared a premature
glass of white wine.
                    "I'll walk you downstairs."
                                        "Sure."
Out on the dim landing, you pushed the door
shut behind us, one hand on the small
of my back, then, pushed me back against the wall
hung with winter coats. I almost slipped
in the half-dark; half-gasped as you unzipped
my pants and tugged them down, silencing my
exclamation with your tongue, your thigh
opening mine. I grabbed your ass with one
hand, hair with the other. You began
stroking my belly, but I pulled you close
against me, covering what you'd exposed.
You whispered, "Should I get down on my knees
and lick you?"
                "No, with your hand, like that, there, please!"
Mouth on your mouth, I rode you, barely stand-
ing up, or standing it. You moved your hand
past where I put it, through the parting, wet
for you already, spread me, and I let
you deep in, while your lips went soft beneath
my mouth, and I tasted salt behind your teeth.
Your fingers brought the juices down around
what swelled into your palm, until you found
where it would come from. Inches of my bare
skin burned against your jeans. Into your hair
I pleaded, "Let me," but you wouldn't; pulled
a centimeter back, instead. The chill
air on my skin pulsed through me like a smack,
and, for a breath, I let my head fall back

against the linen sleeves and woolen folds,
then drew you onto me, so I could hold
myself up to your kisses, while you took
me, out and in, with your whole hand. I shook,
off balance, needed it, you, just there. I
thrust up against you. Then my inner thigh
muscles convulsed, and I bore down on you,
wrenching out "Now!" as heat arrowed into
the place you had me, till I couldn't stop
it coming, crushed against you, half on top
of you, or you on me, breathed through your lips
a huge, collapsing sigh. Arms round my hips,
holding my ass, you kissed me as I hung
on your shoulders, prodded my hair back with your tongue.
You covered me till I recovered my
balance, and my butt, to say, "Good-bye."
"Call you later."
                    "Ummm." Buttoned, I pushed
away, blinking, stepped back. "I've got to rush!"
and watched my footing down three rickety
flights toward twilight traffic in Chelsea.

James Laughlin

THE MIRROR GIRL

There was a mad old man
who was crazy about be-

ing in love all his life
he had pursued love but

never found it quite as
he wished it to be what

he really wanted was a
mirror girl who was al-

so himself he hoped to
look into her eyes and

see himself but he never
found her they all want-

ed to be themselves this
sad & mad old man search-

ing for his mirror girl
right up to the very end.

WHY DO YOU NEVER ENTER MY DREAMS?

Nightly I await you
but you do not come

the lamp burns the
table is spread the

Falernian is decanted
yet it is dawn and you

have not appeared are
you afraid of my dreams

they are loving & will
not harm you or is it

that in sleep you visit
the dreams of another?

Debora Iyall

I GET A BATH

You lift shanks of emerald succulents to scrub the slope
of my rocky, monumental back.
A hiker stuck in the mud
You try, but do not succeed
to scrub off the starfish wedged in my crevices.
Heavy on the top, I was one of the first cliffs fallen
an island off the mainland
My lower half below the wind.
Do your lizard blue eyes know their scaly
history?
Water hatches anything
that falls from me.

UNTITLED

I am waiting, on the outside
And what is outside,
Won't wait for me.

Under tule fog the
Brilliant orange leaves of
Peach trees in autumn
Have turned into shopping malls.

I remember the smell of autumn and
Here, it doesn't reach me.

Light filters through the debris in the airwell.

I've made a name for myself
But my name is not alive
It has no scent.

ON ANOTHER DAY

There on the sidewalk will
Rest the drill that
Competes with the
Melody of the piano

On another day the
Oasis on television
will be
Right outside my window

Wind will blow
Dropping dates into my hands
That are the
Color of dates

I'll open a music box
and the music will
Leap onto paper
Emerald, shocking pink and
Taxi yellow.

On another day
I won't smell like
Spiderwebs and the ants won't
March to their death
In my sink.
We will sing
Anyplace we want to.

On yet another day
There will be a party
The people whose eyes
Glisten

When you walk into the room
Will be there
Because it thrills them to
See you on your birthday!
Because on this day
it thrills us to see you.

For Martha on her Birthday!

Roland Topor

Tom Clark

FRIEDRICH & THE BEYOND

Considering the hyaline
liquidity
which in the extremely
deep spaces
of their backgrounds
are like swimming pools
filled up not with water
but with light
it could be said of Friedrich's canvases
that at first the lens
of the viewer
leans out on Infinity
while a second glance
opens the floodgates to Existence
which closes in all around
from the edges of the picture

When he worked
at painting a sky
no one was permitted
to enter his studio
because he believed
God was present

Alongside the Baltic
grey translucent light
fell on the lake of oil
that formed on the vertical
wall of the canvas
on the other side
there was nothing at all

BLACK SATURDAY

In the spring borne aloft on green skies
And rough trade winds, the kind that always buoy me,
I dropped down into black cities,
My soul's insides papered with chilly statements yet to be uttered.

I exposed myself to dogs on black streets
I pumped black water into myself, heard black screams of lost souls
But all that, reader, still left me cold
and empty, giddy and lightheaded as before.

They knocked holes out through my walls
These things I kept inside me, they poured out
Proving there was nothing inside me but space
And silence—all I was was paper, so they swore.

I kept on falling, smiling, falling—between homes
Of men, out through drains into open country. Winds
Jet-streamed through my walls, now they had it easy
And in came the rain, and in came the snow.

Finally every barfly for miles could inform you
Without lifting snout from trough: there's nothing to me
But this voidzone mudpigs roll around in, down upon
Which birds drip slime from a milky sky.

Less substance in me than in that lowering sky!
Less than in the wind that slices through! I traveled on
Wings of my own poetry following a stork
Much swifter than myself, eastward toward dawn.

Wife One in Country

LYDIA DAVIS

Wife one calls to speak to son. Wife two answers with impatience, gives phone to son of wife one. Son has heard impatience in voice of wife two and tells mother he thought caller was father's sister: raging aunt, constant caller, troublesome woman. Wife one wonders: is she herself perhaps another raging woman, constant caller? No, raging woman but not constant caller. Though for wife two, also troublesome woman.

After speaking to son, much disturbance in wife one. Wife one misses son, also thinks of how some years ago she too answered phone and talked to husband's raging sister, constant caller, protecting husband from troublesome woman. Now wife two protects husband from troublesome sister, constant caller, and also from wife one, raging woman. Wife one sees this and imagines future wife three protecting husband not only from raging wife one but also troublesome wife two, as well as constantly calling sister.

After speaking to son, wife one, often raging though now quiet woman, eats dinner alone though in company of large television. Wife one swallows food, swallows pain, swallows food again, swallows pain again, swallows food. Watches intently ad about easy-to-clean stove: mother who is not real mother flips fried egg onto hot burner, then fries second egg and gives cheerful young son who is not real son loving kiss as spaniel who is not real family dog steals second fried egg off plate of son who is not real son. Wife one swallows food, swallows pain, watches intently mother who is not real mother with son who is not real son. Pain increases in wife one, wife one swallows food, swallows pain, swallows food, swallows pain, swallows food, swallows pain.

Foucault and Pencil

LYDIA DAVIS

Sat down to read Foucault with pencil in hand. Knocked over glass of water onto waiting room floor. Put down Foucault and pencil, mopped up water, refilled glass. Sat down to read Foucault with pencil in hand. Stopped to write note in notebook. Took up Foucault with pencil in hand. Counsellor beckoned from doorway. Put away Foucault and pencil as well as notebook and pen. Sat with counsellor discussing situation fraught with conflict taking form of many heated arguments. Counsellor pointed to danger, raised red flag. Left counsellor, went to subway. Sat in subway car, took out Foucault and pencil but did not read, thought instead about situation fraught with conflict, red flag, recent argument concerning travel: argument itself became form of travel, each sentence carrying arguers on to next sentence, next sentence on to next, and in the end, arguers were not where they had started, were also tired from travelling and spending so long face to face in each other's company. After several stations on subway thinking about argument, stopped thinking and opened Foucault. Found Foucault, in French, hard to understand. Short sentences easier to understand than long ones. Certain long ones understandable part by part, but so long, forgot beginning before reaching end. Went back to beginning, understood beginning, read on, and again forgot beginning before reaching end. Read on without going back and without understanding, pencil idle in hand. Read on without understanding, without remembering, and without learning. Came to sentence that was clear, made pencil mark in margin. Mark indicated understanding, indicated forward progress in book. Lifted eyes from Foucault, looked at other passengers. Took out notebook and pen to make note about passengers, made accidental mark with pencil in margin of Foucault, put down notebook, erased mark. Returned thoughts to argument. Argument not only like vehicle, carried arguers forward, but also like plant, grew like hedge, surrounding arguers at first thinly, some light coming through, then more thickly, keeping light out, or darkening light. By argument's end, arguers could not leave hedge, could not leave each other, and light was dim. Thought of question to ask about argument, took out notebook and pen and wrote down. Put away notebook and returned to Foucault. Understood more clearly at which points Foucault harder to understand and at which points easier: harder to understand when sentence was long and noun identifying subject of sentence was left back at beginning, replaced by male or female pronoun, when forgot what noun pronoun replaced and had only pronoun for company travelling through sentence. Sometimes that pronoun then giving way in mid-sentence to new noun, new noun in turn replaced by new pronoun which then continued on to end of sentence. Also harder to understand when subject of sentence was noun like thought, absence, law; easier to understand when subject was noun like beach, wave, sand, sanitorium, pension, door, hallway, or civil servant. Before and after sentence about sand, civil servant or pension, however, came sentence about attraction, neglect, or sentence about emptiness, absence, and law, so parts of book understood stood unconnected like islands. Put down Foucault and pencil, took out notebook and made note of what was now at least understood about lack of understanding reading Foucault, looked up at other passengers, thought again about argument, made note of same question about argument as before though with stress on different word.

A Night in Tunisia

MICHAEL WOLFE

She phoned at five and caught him at the office. Can you come to talk to me tonight? she asked. I have to talk to you. I'll make you dinner. Or have you forgotten all about me.

He hadn't heard a word from her since August. Now she couldn't wait to see his face. Was he supposed to drop his work and rush right over? He didn't think so. He decided not to answer. Last summer she had had him on a string, then left things hanging. If silence made her nervous, she deserved it. He couldn't tell what this was all about, but when he heard her strike a match, then blow a stream of smoke against the mouthpiece, he enjoyed his new position for a moment.

When she spoke again, he knew it was a joke. I can see you at your desk, he heard her whisper.

It had to be a joke. Her house, across the bay, lay thirty miles from where he worked and had an unobstructed view of the horizon. Though on evenings when the sky was very clear there, you could spot his office building from her porch, it never looked much larger than a toothpick. To claim that she could see him made him laugh.

He hadn't really meant to laugh. As they began to talk, she won him over. Finally he said, All right, I'll come. Take your time, I'll wait for you, she told him. The traffic would be backed up to the bridge now. The drive was going to take about two hours.

He shrugged his shoulders setting down the phone. He had been enough in love with her last year to drive out every weekend to her cottage. She was always glad to see him there, but things were not so serious on her side, and for a while he hid his real feelings. When he told her, he regretted it at once. They were upstairs on the mattress in her loft the night it happened, he could just see Diamond Heights across the bay, and the more he talked the moodier it made her. That was a Sunday. On Tuesday she phoned up and broke it off.

He was over feeling hurt, but he remembered, and he wondered what she wanted with him now. He knew he should have turned her down and not seemed bothered. It wouldn't have required much pretending. After what she'd put him through he didn't think he cared enough for her to hurt him, he didn't see her phone call as a trap, but he was bothered. He squared a stack of papers on his desk and looked them over, upset because of course he felt intrigued. It's because she's from Tunisia, he guessed. It wasn't possible to go on working. He locked the office, went downstairs, and got into his car.

He thought about Tunisia in the traffic. He had gone there after college for a summer, years before, and been so taken by the beauty of its desert that, when the autumn rains began, he found a flat in Sfax and settled down to try his hand at painting. He did not write his parents about this. Nobody at home would have believed it. At Stanford he had studied economics. It would never have occurred to him to paint; only the Sahara could have done it. The landscapes and the light there left him spellbound, and he brought some sketches back with him to Sfax, but before he could get down to work his father passed away in San Francisco, and this inevitably dragged him home.

Economics put an end to these adventures and he never saw Tunisia again. Instead, he went into his father's firm and took it over. Years of working drew him into a routine which he enjoyed now. He had finally stopped lamenting his entrenchment, when this woman came to prove what it had cost. Although they had been introduced as friends, it seemed like fate to find her in his country. She knew that he had seen her homeland once, but never guessed how much it meant, or what her weekends with him represented. When he finally talked to her, she was astonished. She didn't like to be mistaken for a country, or for a private tributary of his youth. She had slept with him because she was a woman, not a painting of a palm tree or a dune. She had dropped him without giving him any reasons; later on, he saw the thing for what it was, a desperate passion he had failed to recover, not a passion for a person but a place. He thought about it as he crossed the city. He imagined she had called him up tonight to talk about it over dinner. Now that it was done, they should be able to talk calmly. He could almost hear their voices as he drove.

He fought through rush-hour traffic to the bridge, crossed the bay, and climbed the mountain road. Behind some redwoods on a cliff the winter sun dropped down on the Pacific, then a sickle moon came up and bathed the coast. He knew the narrow, hairpin curves by heart now. He forgot the stack of papers on his desk, turned on the radio, and thought of nothing. When he passed a pair of deer he swerved, and went on up the ridge, and then the music faded into static, and the bright lights of the city sprawled behind him like a pitcher full of stars spilled on the earth. He wondered if they looked that way from her place. He watched them in the mirror as he drove.

The blacktop leveled out again beside a long lagoon, then heavy fog rolled in over the highway. He drove the last few miles very quickly and nearly missed the turnoff to her house. A silver car with foreign plates sat in the driveway. He could not recall it being there before. He parked behind it, doused his lights, and killed the engine.

The windows on the porch were glowing faintly as he climbed the steps. He peeked in at the door, and saw two candles burning on a table. Between them sat a wooden salad bowl, bones on white plates smeared with sparerib sauce, and half a fifth of brandy. The meal she had promised him was over. He checked his watch and couldn't read the dial. His eyes picked up an outline of the ladder in the hallway and followed it up to the bedroom loft. The candles flickered. Then a pair of naked feet came down the rungs. He recognized her bathrobe in the shadows. He heard *Shuffle Boil* on the stereo, it was a record he had given her last summer, and then she eased her way toward the table, splashed a shot of brandy in a glass, and climbed with it in one hand to the loft. The cold air made one eye tear as he stared into the rafters. His hand was on the glass, about to knock, when down the ladder came a tall, young girl. Her hair was longer than the other woman's, it swayed and caught the light as she came down and stood out first against the dark, because she was a blonde. He couldn't see much more as she descended, until she stood with both feet on the floor. When she turned to face the door, he didn't know her. When she stepped into the light, his mind went blank. She had no clothes on. The fine down on her belly gleamed as she advanced toward the candles. Her hair slid off one shoulder as she bent to pinch them out, but before she straightened up again he lost her. Darkness fell inside the house.

He stole back to the car and slipped the handbrake, rolled downhill before he turned the key, and drove back to the city very quickly. When the radio came into range, he turned it to the football scores, and listened to them until he reached the bridge. In town, the silent streets outside his office were lined with parked cars up and down for blocks. He had to drive around for twenty minutes, before he finally found a place to park.

The Czarina Complex

JANET RICHARDS

She had started very far back, Gwyneth Jones, granddaughter of a Welsh immigrant bookkeeper, and she had a long way to go.

It had begun with youth, that condition of rattled naiveté, which appeared to have a triumph when she fell violently in love with Gerald Silvestri. She was one of six hundred young women in his Philosophy 101 lecture course for freshmen at Columbia.

Statistical nonsense it was; but, as destiny created by human character it had stunning justness.

One could consider the question of why she had not fallen in love with her history professor, a poetically handsome bachelor, younger by ten years than Gerald.

To create a destiny there must be two people's participation if it is a matter of a love affair. Therefore it was inevitable that once, in the hallway when they passed each other, Gerald should stop her with a hand on her arm and say, "Aren't you in my Philosophy 101 class?"

This was Gwyneth's first coup in life, and she almost lost the power of speech. Yet she managed to say normally, "Yes, I am."

He laughed, as one does at a child. He could afford a moment's fatherly abatement of his famous magnetic sexuality. "Well, how do you like it?"

"Oh, I love it!" she said, much too fervently. She knew as soon as the words were out that she had lost his interest.

He gave her one long look, then nodded and passed on down the hall. In those moments of anguished regret she matured extraordinarily.

Gerald Silvestri was not exactly famous. One cannot become famous as a philosopher, as one can become famous as an actor. To become a "Philosopher" one must move in a realm of originality so rare only a couple of a dozen people will be found there. However, Gerald had published a book on aesthetics that was very well known, widely studied, considered a contribution to this vexed area of philosophy, and was used as a textbook not only here but at other universities. And he had a simply local fame as Columbia's charmer, and as one of the top prizes of its current staff.

Gwyneth had intended to major in English, because she had already written some stories that avoided amateurism, chiefly by being innocuous. But she had shown the acumen characteristic of her when she began her really serious writing with a biography, knowing that her experience of life was too limited to make her fiction interesting. Her choice of subject had not been adroit, however, and was what sank the book in the end. She had chosen Christopher Marlowe. Whatever had made her suppose she could contribute anything to the literature about this mysterious, flashing and supremely sophisticated sixteenth-century person? As she floundered in the bogs of the mystifications surrounding Marlowe, and her own inability to make cohesive and intelligible her intuitions about him (which were what was good in her efforts), she gradually shortened her projected book from a standard length to a sort of poetic novella, half history, half girlish enthusiasm. In her junior year she simply threw it all in the trash one afternoon, when common sense convinced her that here were 150 weak pages of no interest.

But by the time she had acquired this sure ability to make a judgment based on common sense, she had changed her major from English to philosophy. She had shown a gift for philosophy, but essentially she was quite methodically in pursuit of Gerald.

Now she had passed through the fires of Sartre and had been cleansed of cliché and Platonic residue. She had philosophical grounds for what she had always more secretly thought about herself: that she was one who would do as she pleased.

"Do you know anybody with enough time to type up some notes for me, Alfred?" she heard the well-known, low, peculiarly subjugating voice ask as she sat consulting with her instructor in his tiny office, and looked up to see Gerald's tall figure relaxed against the door jamb, dominated by his tousle of gray hair and his greenish eyes, creased at the corners as he smiled. He smiled at her, not at Alfred.

"Oh, hello Gerald. This is Miss Jones. Come on in."

"How do you do, Miss Jones," said Gerald, sitting down and putting his tanned and rather wrinkled hands on his knees. Erect and lithe, he had the look of somebody who has just climbed down from a long ascent up a mountain. "And what is the other part that goes with the 'Jones?'"

"Gwyneth."

"My God, you are Welsh. Still, it could be worse. So you went on in philosophy, did you?"

She was under an enchantment. He was wooing her. She smiled, and her cheeks grew pink. She had a dazzling smile, so unexpected in her brooding, rather heavy face with its crown of dark hair, that the effect was of a revelation, as if a hand had swept the heavens clear of gray clouds and brought forth the sun.

Alfred saw that Gerald had stopped at his door because Gwyneth was sitting in his office and was now smiling dazzling smiles. Alfred had never seen dazzling smiles and therefore he took a place as a member of an audience.

"I don't really know why I went into it," Gwyneth said. "I don't plan to teach."

"Philosophy will teach you how to die," remarked Gerald.

"I have also learned how to type," she continued smoothly.

"Splendid girl. Would you like to type up some notes for me? I pay, of course."

"But of course I'd be delighted," she meant to show her regard for his eminence.

"You could come along now and I'll hand it over. If you have time."

She had time. They rose and together, he tall and athletic but thickened a little with middle age, she also tall, but slender and smooth. As they walked away Alfred watched them sardonically.

It was only a short walk to the crosstown bus, and in what seemed merely minutes she was meeting Renee, his small, dark French wife, with her plain face and spontaneous manner, his daughter Heloise, a crude, hostile teenager, the three Siamese cats, who sat leaning together on top of a tall chest as if they were one animal, and most of all his beloved East River flat, a series of small rooms opening into one another, from which, she later came to feel, Gerald could be torn only if tied to a horse. His son Marc was not home.

Gwyneth thought the flat was graceless, French bourgeois, decorative platitudes, but she had already mastered the perjorative art of damning with faint praise and her naive exclamations were very deceptive. Finally she was sitting beside the tiny living room fireplace where a pretty little fire burned on this chilly spring day, chatting easily with Renee over a cup of good India tea, while Gerald muttered noisily from his study, where he was collecting the material for her to type.

She and Renee had established an instant rapport.

Gwyneth stayed only about ten minutes after Gerald came back with a bundle of handwritten pages. By this time he and she were on such a level of sexual response to each other that it was becoming obvious. She knew she must get away. She was able to think of nothing coherently on her way home, as her triumphant emotions carried her through the streets on their own.

After an hour of regaining her poise in her room, she realized that she felt like a medical student who had just gone through the experience of taking the Hippocratic oath. Thousands of young women at Columbia would wish to capture the prize of Gerald Silvestri.

In a week she left a message at his office to the effect that she had finished the typing. He had asked her particularly not to leave the work itself there.

He telephoned. He would come for it, after a meeting that night, about ten.

That night she saw Gerald at his best. After they had sat and talked briefly about what she had typed, he merely rose, without haste, took her hand in his own, relaxed, warm hand, raised her upright, and without solemnity or anything fake, simply walked with her into the bedroom, where he held her loosely against him, quietly, until her heart stopped pounding, and their blood seemed to flow together. His demeanor was so direct that he gathered about him the dignity of natural things, a rock or a waterfall, and at the same time he was the quintessence of all that is most moving and beautiful about masculinity.

Their first night together was nothing special. She remembered that he threw the hairpins he took out of her long hair one by one over the back of the bed onto the floor.

Gerald was brilliant as a theorist, even as a theorist of psychology, but he hadn't the knack of understanding real people. What he had was an uncanny ability to recognize the one exactly right person for the right moment, and it was this ability that had turned him toward Gwyneth.

Not even in the morning did they descend from the heights of elitism they had tacitly agreed they were on. For example, they didn't mention Renee. It might be noted that Renee, in the same position, would have done the same. After breakfast they went back to bed. His sexual reputation had been earned, Gwyneth found, not to her surprise. Her own appetite was rather under her control. Now she gave it full liberty. As a result, their sexual harmony became for her a truth to which she became passionately loyal.

She retained her little student's apartment, but essentially she became a member of a family group consisting of Gerald, Renee, herself, Heloise, Marc, the cats, the East River and the parties. Columbia talked about little else for awhile, and their arrangements remained a standard focus for small talk and gossip. But after absorbing Camus, Genet, de Beauvoir, Gwyneth was not much affected by the social lies that she felt stood between people and freedom, much as a window pane imprisons the fly, whose wisdom has not yet penetrated the mendacious secret of glass. Gerald ineffably referred to Gwyneth as his secretary.

The children counted for little. They had in early childhood counted themselves out, in fact, making the choice they had—to attach their emotional interests to their peers and to school rather than to their parents—to save themselves from psychological ruin. Heloise was now enthralled by algebra (she became a physicist), and Marc dawdled about, as yet undirected and unformed. When their parents made occasional forays in their direction they easily slid away, and a week's confinement to their rooms was the worst that ever happened. Gwyneth seemed to them only another boring adult in the house.

Renee was unique. She was devoid of the passion of jealousy (Gwyneth was not). She liked Gwyneth. Besides, Gwyneth became amazingly useful. Renee would have taken it for granted that Gerald's girl would be useful in typing work for him free of charge, but when she found that Gwyneth could not cook at all but actually rather enjoyed the monotonous work of chopping shallots, carrots, celery, and measuring out precise cups of flour, she was truly joyful. Renee was a very fine cook, though she could cook nothing that wasn't French. But then, if it wasn't French Renee would not have supposed it to be fit to cook, let alone eat. It was her Sauce Nantua, her Potatoes Anna, her succulent peasant cassoulets that had cost Gerald his youthful slimness, which had earlier made him the finest figure of a man seen at Columbia on a lecture platform in decades. Or so it was claimed, with malicious intent by the disenchanted who had known him for years.

And occasionally Renee now took pleased advantage of handy Gwyneth, and would absent herself without explanation for two or three weeks, leaving the flat, the parties, Gerald, the children and the cats in Gwyneth's care. Gerald always railed the whole time at her shallow Gallic high-handedness, but it was all only a front for the suffering Gwyneth caused him with her idea of what consti-tuted a meal. Unless it was canned black bean soup, it came from the corner Chinese restaurants in cartons.

Gwyneth did not like the cats, but these cats did not like people, so it was of no importance. Nervous at first, she finally got accustomed to their strange-ness, with their inexplicable races through the flat and their silent, motionless clustering on top of the high chest, a heap of entwined, densely furred beige bodies lit by six incandescent eyes.

Gwyneth's significant alienation began some time in the second year—ultimate alienation had been put into the equation from its first formulation.

Gwyneth had always, both publicly and privately, been testing Gerald's eru-dition for authenticity. She had never been able to detect anything amiss with it. Yet it was on an academic matter that she first decided to leave him.

It was because he had refused to give a recommendation to a graduate student for a small instructorship. When she had furiously inquired why, Gerald had explained to her, step by step, where the boy's work was deficient. He was right. But Gwyneth knew Gerald might have bent his strict assessment had he chosen, because the boy's faults were minor and probably temporary.

The point for Gwyneth was that this boy worshipped Gerald, had been taken into the household to run errands and to listen, enraptured, as Gerald held forth, that he took the car to the mechanic and brought it back, and in actuality had become Gerald's willing slave.

When Gwyneth contemptuously pointed all this out to Gerald, he shrugged and said, "The more fool he, then." At that she left the flat, flinging on her coat at the door, and took a plane to Pittsburgh, where her married friend Valerie lived.

Valerie had also remained, after graduation, in the academic world, though on a more conventional basis. Her husband was a geologist who taught at Pitts-burgh University. He was insignificant to the point of being ostentatiously so. Gwyneth did not ask, but since she assumed that no friend of hers could do other than despise the geologist, she assumed that Valerie did despise him.

Roland Topor

As if they had merely been away on summer vacation, Gwyneth and Valerie picked up their relationship exactly where they had left it in college, and began doing all the things they had done when they lived in a dormitory. They did not talk about the geologist or Gerald. They went to afternoon movies and concerts, and had scotches in hotel bars later. Gwyneth offered no explanation for her having left Gerald but she did enter into a conspiracy with Valerie to be on the lookout for Geraldic onslaughts. One rule was to hang up whenever he called. Another was not to answer the doorbell.

Yet, somehow a screaming Gerald had got around Valerie, and one day when Gwyneth returned to the house Gerald was there. It ended in her sullen return to the East River flat.

Renee's welcome was exactly what Gwyneth would have expected, and in fact had counted on. "Thank God for that," she exclaimed, after kissing her briefly. "You can't imagine what it's been like around here."

"What did Gerald actually do?" Gwyneth asked, in a rare exposure of her secret concerns.

"He screamed," said Renee. "Let us have tea."

Life returned to its former condition. Gwyneth was very reluctant to turn her back on their passion. She believed that passion was absolutely pure, as Sir Galahad had believed the Holy Grail to be, that it alone justified Man's existence and his restraint from suicide, and that it discharged with its might every blood-ied debt mankind owed the earth.

Yet it did not escape her intelligence that she had had a better time bumming around Pittsburgh with Valerie than she had had in years.

So she looked up Isabel, her second best college friend, who now lived in Brooklyn Heights with her three small children, having left their rich, dilettante-lawyer father. Movie matinees with Isabel and rum colas (it was now summer) afterward were as much fun with Isabel as they had been with Valerie. Nobody ever knew where she went in the afternoons, but when she and Isabel began taking courses in art history, Chinese art, and music of the Baroque, she began to discuss art and music with Gerald and Renee. Gerald knew all about painting and what, theoretically, made it good, but it did not move him. Yet Renee, whose education had consisted of a year and a half of idling at the Sorbonne, could understand a painting and could love it.

Gwyneth considered these facts with care. Just as in the beginning she had determined to conquer Gerald, so now, after Gerald's betrayal of the student he had befriended, she had determined to map out the territory of Gerald's fraudulency.

She had not yet decided what she really wanted to do (there was much about her situation, with its peculiar eminence, that she still liked), and so her stalking of Gerald as an imposter was an amusement to make life in the flat at least have some interest while she chopped carrots and carried out the myriad domesticities that accompany sharing a domicile.

She had no desire to conceal her new skepticism. Shrewd Gerald took it all in at a glance, and went her one better: he began to expose her weaknesses, and he was heavily armed. First he neatly laid bare her own inability to love paintings, a truth that annoyed her, and so the time passed, with great improvement in her fighting spirit.

Gerald's parties were traditions. People have rather shaky allegiance to traditions, and it was often merely for form's sake that some professors attended a couple of times a year. Students attended eagerly, glad to get a foot up the ladder. Only the young instructors came in any sense freely, and with these young men Gwyneth found amusement. They all reminded her of Alfred (now an assistant professor at Yale), in whose office she and Gerald had met.

The parties wandered all over the long, narrow flat, from the East River windows to the pantry behind the kitchen, where fairly often dalliances were consummated. Gerald held forth in his study, surrounded by spellbound students and such visiting dignitaries as were in New York for academic purposes. In the three front rooms there was music and dancing, or sitting and talking. Gwyneth never went near the study. Renee being hostess, it was she who saw that there was always sufficient wine and the cheapest bourbon.

Gwyneth loved dancing, the more so because Gerald held it to be a diversion in the same category as musical chairs or post office, especially the latter, because, as he said, "dancing leads to kissing, and kissing leads to the pantry."

When she chose, Gwyneth could make her dark, sulky personality and heavy face come alive, and with her brilliant smile enchant men. The young instructors were surprised to find her so attractive. They most often heard in the gossip that she was dreary.

So she and the instructors danced and flirted. To this defiant independence, Gwyneth added a new and delicious game of fencing with the instructors to see who could come the closest to laughing openly at Gerald and still remain beyond specific reproach. Their methods took the odd form that is recommended in the little instruction book for the paranoid Far Right on how to trip up the enemy by putting your point in the form of a polite question.

Ironically enough, it was in this dancing which Gerald laughed at, that Gwyneth found her next experiment. She decided to take a lover.

She was attracted to a student, an intense, very dark and smoldering Zionist, and they had an affair, a few meetings in his dank, dirty apartment that he shared with a girl who was about to leave for Israel. Finally he simply stopped calling her, never came to the parties, and quite soon joined the girl in Israel. Gwyneth was dissatisfied with this adventure, though its crudeness strongly appealed to her.

Promiscuity did not seem the direction she fancied. It was not really compatible with marriage, or with a permanent liaison like hers. Yet she was still restless, still highly alert and watchful for possibilities among the large number of young men who came to the parties.

She had a predilection for dark, Semitic men, and in a few weeks became interested in such a one, a musician named Paul. He was so absorbed in music and took so little time for girls that Gwyneth's charms, which were considerable when she chose them to be, bowled him over and easily aroused his normal sexual needs, somewhat neglected. He lustfully offered to give her a few piano lessons to see if she might want to study the piano to alleviate what she told him was her boredom.

Nothing escaped Gerald, who could pay attention to several things at once, and in his furious jealousy he began to snarl at her about her perversities. They fought bitterly.

Paul was a most charming person, sweet, naive, indifferent to her conjugal status (or anybody's), and now that he was turned on, exceedingly passionate. Gwyneth's femininity was flattered, her own appetites were aroused, and she began to glow with excitement. She wrote some poems in celebration of Paul.

She decided on an elopement. "What's the matter with things as they are?" Paul objected, startled and worried. "I'm right in the middle of my Schoenberg study!"

She wanted to leave Gerald, she told him; she must leave Gerald. She could no longer stand the sham, the role-playing, the storms, she was wasting her life—and she loved him. She was not asking him to commit himself, only to help her get away, to break out. She found getting Paul to agree to this was the most difficult part of the whole enterprise, much harder than fooling Gerald. But finally Paul said he would go with her.

Furious as Gerald could become, and as violent, Gwyneth was taking no risks, as she well knew, because between them, she and Renee were barely sufficient to fill Gerald's enormous need to be attended to. He would always take her back when she chose to come.

So, blithely she got on the train to Pittsburgh with Paul, and they took refuge with Valerie, who was so adaptable.

But in four days Paul gave her a dreadful shock. Gwyneth had simply had no idea of the kind of hold music has on musicians. It had never occurred to her that Valerie had no piano. But when Paul found this out, he was staggered, and began a decline from which he did not rise again, as far as Gwyneth was concerned. Paul began then, without a piano, to think about what he was doing.

He found himself irritated by the airless, dusty atmosphere of the flat in Pittsburgh, by Valerie and her inane husband. Worse, he grew more and more disgusted by Gwyneth's long girlish chats with Valerie and their plots about not answering the doorbell and hanging up the phone when Gerald called. But everything fell to pieces for him when he discovered that Gwyneth had almost entirely lost interest in him when she had arrived at the flat.

He kept all this to himself, and for three nights they lay apart in their sagging bed in their cubbyhole of a bedroom. On the fourth morning, after a silent cup of coffee by himself, he took Gwyneth back into the cubbyhole and standing with his back against the closed door said, "Will you please tell me what is going on? What is it I'm supposed to be part of?" He glared, and his voice rose. "I thought you wanted to leave Gerald. You don't want to leave Gerald at all. You only think about what's happening at Columbia. How about what's happening here, to me?" He became very excited as the reaction to the crowded experience of the past weeks found explosive utterance. "You came here to giggle with Valerie, and play games. You're childish. How many other men have you done this to? And who the hell do you think you are, the real Anastasia?"

She laughed insultingly at him. He slapped her. She hissed at him. "Baby!" He seized his shaving kit and extra socks lying on the bureau, dumped them into his canvas bag, and with not so much as a glance at Valerie, banged the front door shut and returned to New York, where for two days he played Beethoven until he felt like a man again.

Gwyneth instantly dismissed this man from further attention: he had failed to take in the point. Consequently, when the door banged, she collapsed with laughter on the sofa. Coincidentally the phone rang.

It was Renee, and Valerie talked to her. Gwyneth paid heed. Renee was a serious person, too wise in the ways of Gerald to be easily manipulated. Renee was vehement, and as Valerie held the phone outward into the room Gwyneth could hear her.

"... and not only that but the cats all caught feline pneumonia and have died. Gerald is trying to make me come to Pittsburgh. Of course I won't. But Gwyneth must come home. This is too much and I won't stand it."

"The cats," Gwyneth gasped, doubled over with wild laughter. When she could at last stop laughing she made herself a large scotch, meditated on Renee's declaration, which she understood for what it was, a threat, and went back that night.

Gerald raged for an hour, on high moral grounds concerning sanctities that Gerald insisted were inherent in family life. Gwyneth knew it was all only a defense of the status quo, and womanish jealousy. She gave him his hour, and without saying anything at all, went to bed.

This time life did not go on quite as before, though Gerald's sanctities were preserved. At any rate everybody was still under one roof. The conditions under which they were seemed to be of no account to Gerald; it was the fact that was important.

But Gwyneth was growing restless. It no longer amused her to watch Gerald using people—Renee, herself, the children, students, whoever was willing and dumb enough to be used. It rather took all the fun out of it to know, as she finally did, that Gerald could perfectly well do for himself everything these minions did for him and in all cases do it better. Moreover, he whistled as he worked—while, for example, he prepared a meal when Renee was not there. It was more difficult to get the best of Gerald than anybody supposed, even those who were wise to his ways. In the end he always came out possessing inarguable rightness. Had he had any heart he would have been a great man.

She was no longer interested.

She began to put money away into a savings account. Money was easy to come by in that house. Gerald made a large salary, far exceeding their needs. Renee's clothes were expensive and elegant, but she felt no need to have many of them. Gerald never spent money on anything, as it bought him very little he desired.

When Gwyneth left she did nothing, as she had done before. She was in touch with no one. She took a room in a luxurious hotel, though she did not change her name. She would never do that.

She liked her room exceedingly well, and moved slowly about among its bogus splendors. She would buy some pale pink wax roses, and let her senses delight in their perfection and in their bizarre destiny—they could not die.

Even the Mona Lisa, upon whose care the French government spends millions of francs, is dying; even the Parthenon, over whose part of Athens no aircraft is permitted passage, is dying. People will give their lives for the Mona Lisa, for the Parthenon.

But she thought she would live for the degenerate sensations in a wax rose. For a while.

That night she dressed carefully in a slate-blue silk suit that enhanced her slender figure, wore the high-heeled plastic shoes she had bought the day before, and went to the bar.

She spent the night with the fourth man who tried to pick her up, and when he left in the morning she told him that if he wished to see her again it would cost him five hundred dollars. He did not come back, but the third man she spent the night with did.

Political Poetry and Formalist Avant-Gardes

Four Viewpoints

ADAM CORNFORD: JAMES BROOK: IAIN BOAL: TOM CLARK

> Does so-called political poetry have a political-agitational effect on its readers? Are the connections between formalist avant-gardes and their associated political tendencies purely fortuitous? Is the opposition between "formalist" writing and "content-oriented" writing false, real, productive or unproductive? What of the relationships, if any, between poetry and social revolution, or poetry and the transformation of life?

ADAM CORNFORD:

"Political poetry," obviously, covers a very wide field. This field has widened steadily during the last two centuries, as previously disenfranchised or extra-literate groups (groups outside mainstream literary and cultural activity) have begun to produce poetry at the same time as they have expanded the bounds of "politics" itself. In the seventeenth century, a political poem was about rulers and affairs of state—Marvell's ode on Cromwell, for instance. Only popular songs and radical Protestant hymns, generally not written down until much later if at all, indicated the beginnings of "politics from below." With the Romantics the proto-political ballad tradition linked up for the first time with literature, both via working-class writers reaching up to appropriate elite poetic discourse (Blake) and via middle-class writers consciously imitating popular forms (Wordsworth, Shelley).

Analogous dialectics continue to this day as Black American and Caribbean poets, Chicano-Latino and Nuyorican poets, feminist, lesbian and gay poets, all have sought to politicize poetry from their own vantage points. Typically, this process begins with often crudely polemical outpourings of anger, frustration and revolutionary hope, mingled with flashes of brilliant insight and poetic vigor. In this way a field of discourse and a readership are created. Slowly, critical standards are defined beyond the raw, denotative "correctness" of the work; space is opened up for ambivalence and ambiguity, for formal experimentation and complex personal statement. An acknowledged ranking of talent and achievement begins to appear, and some stars gain recognition outside the group (Imamu Baraka, Adrienne Rich, Ntozake Shange, Gary Soto, Miguel Pineda ...).

As the writing becomes more sophisticated, however, the wide audience within the group tends to dry up. The radical potential of the initial angry upsurge is dissipating, as questioning of the existing order devolves to demanding equal participation and recognition within it. When this demand is partially granted, at least on the level of representation, the thirst for "voice," for a discourse or language field that expresses the actual experience of the group, is partially satisfied. The level of cultural mobilization falls, along with the level of reading. Meanwhile, the poetry's growing sophistication tends to exclude uneducated readers (who in the case of Blacks or Chicanos make up the overwhelming bulk of the population).

It seems, then, that in the "heroic" phase of these literatures, poetry often does have a directly mobilizing effect. It validates the day-to-day experience of members of the group as well as their anger and aspirations (the circu-

lation of the early Chicano poetry anthology *Espejo espejo* among working-class Chicanos is a case in point). Once this phase is over, poetry becomes more like what it is in mainstream (middle-class hetero/white) circles—a very minoritarian medium, kept alive by a handful of increasingly sophisticated writers and a slightly larger handful of aspiring poets and marginal intellectuals who buy the publications and attend the readings.

Generally, it seems that poetry can have a political-agitational effect under two closely related sets of conditions: first, among people who are for some reason marginal to capitalism's organization of appearances, who are not represented as part of its money-community, whether because they live in "underdeveloped" regions or under bureaucratic dictatorships, or because they are an exploited or discriminated-against subgroup in a developed country; and then, among such dispossessed or exploited groups as they are constituting themselves socially and politically, removing themselves to some extent from the grip of the ruling organization of appearances and thereby creating their own public sphere.

●

After 1945 this radical tension in formalist modernism disappeared as the new global economic order, dominated by the USA, evolved adequate political and cultural forms. Modernism lost its critical and utopian content; its once-novel artistic techniques—rapid shifts of tone and breakdowns of syntax, communication via montage of images rather than via rational argument—were adopted by advertising and mass culture. This defeat was accelerated, I believe, because formalisms share deep underlying tendencies with capitalist development.

First, formalisms, like capitalism, are *desacralizing*. They call into question areas of life and experience that were hitherto regarded as natural, essential, or sacred. Marx and Engels, in a famous passage in the *Communist Manifesto,* pointed out how with the advance of commerce "all that is sacred is profaned, all that is solid melts into air, and man is at last compelled to face with sober senses his conditions of life and his relations with his kind." Thus, for example, the Russian Formalists (a group of linguists closely linked to the Futurists) dared to ask not merely how a given poem achieved its effect by means of rhythm, imagery, and so forth, but *what this effect was in the first place*—what *was* the "poetic emotion" that the Romantic tradition had placed beyond rational analysis?

This leads to the second connection, which is that formalisms are typically *analytic*: they break experience down into small interchangeable units. At the turn of the century, Frederick Taylor, father of "scientific management," overthrew the power of American steelmaking craftsmen by detailing every aspect of their work, so that it could be performed in a fragmentary fashion by semiskilled, low-paid workers. Not long after, the Swiss linguist Ferdinand de Saussure rendered language into written or spoken "signifiers" (made up of units called "phonemes" and "graphemes") that could be arbitrarily assembled into an infinite variety of possible "signifieds" (meanings). This parallels the work of the earlier formalist painter Georges Seurat, whose *pointillisme* attempted to make painting into a science by breaking all images down into small dots of color (an effect later achieved much less laboriously by photolithography). Both of these figures have been profoundly influential among twentieth-century avant-gardes.

Third, formalists are *reifying*: they tend to obscure human agency and to ascribe its results to abstractions or objects. Marx analyzed the fetishism of commodities (and hence of capital). This fetishism lends quasihuman or even superhuman subjectivity (power of action and will) to articles of merchandise and quantities of money, so that they appear to confer subjectivity on their owners; meanwhile, the real human activity that valorizes money and merchandise alike—waged work— disappears or seems unimportant. Prices go up and down, markets grow and shrink, capital flows from one sector to another, all apparently by themselves, while poor mortals struggle to keep up with them. Similarly, formalist avant-gardists have placed such reified abstractions as the "Machine" or the "European Spirit" in command of history, have declared that "language speaks men," or have claimed that "structures" of language and culture evolve according to an internal logic entirely independent of human will.

These connections have led to the banality of post-1945 avant-gardes, emptied now of the ambiguously radical energy possessed by their forebears: a pseudoscientific rhetoric of "experiment" and "research," chilly and obscurantist jargon from which the passions are repressed only to return as ludicrous failures of logic or perception, a hatred of the "personal" alternating with narcissistic obsession about the minutiae of the artist's life, ritual denunciations of a past about which the artist knows little and understands less—and above all, a comically transparent ambition to translate "revolt" into patronage, jobs and conventional success as quickly as possible.

•

The formalist/modernist avant-gardes of 1840-1939 had a more complex and ambiguous relationship to the social movements of their time. In general they were (as Marshall Berman argues in *All That Is Solid Melts Into Air*) attempts to "ride" the wave of capitalist modernization, to create a dialectical relationship with it, as the Romantics had largely failed to do.

Also, in general, the young men (and occasional women) who made up these avant-gardes came from the middle and small capitalist classes. While they rebelled strenuously against the complacency, timidity, and conservatism of these classes, they did so partly by identifying themselves with the surges of capitalist development that were causing such immense polit-ical and social dislocation in their countries.

Here the generalizations tend to break down. In Russia before 1914, where the bourgeoisie was especially weak, sections of the intelligentsia in alliance with the urban working class became the agents of modernization. After a genuinely communist working-class revolt had swept away the Czarist political structures, large-scale, capitalist-type industrialization was carried out by a "Communist" government. Hence the ambiguities of Russian Futurism and Constructivism. Futurism reached aggressively out of the cramped "present" of the urban intelligentsia in both directions—to the undervalued, traditional vernacular of peasant life, and to the techno-dreamworld promised by a mechanization that had only just arrived in Russia. Like their Italian counterparts, the Russian Futurists initially glorified World War One on the basis not only of patriotic sentiment but of a sort of modernist nihilism, which both aesthetized the war and hoped that it would clear the ground for further miraculous transformations.

In the case of the Russians, these fantasies were quickly shattered by the vast and unglamorous misery the war brought to their doorsteps. They came to identify with the revolutionary left. The Italian Futurists, whose country was not seriously damaged, retained their illusions (even though at least one Futurist died on the battlefield). They attached themselves to Mussolini's Blackshirts, who seemed to embody a national dynamism as opposed

Roland Topor

to the feebleness of the liberal bourgeoisie and the internationalism of the Socialist working class.

In the USA and Britain, where the capitalist class was already firmly established and the working-class organizations largely reformist or accommodationist, formalist/modernist revolt was more isolated. The tradition in these countries was Romanticism and liberal humanism—sentimental, rhetorical, muddledly optimistic and high-minded. The likes of Ezra Pound and Wyndham Lewis (who edited the Vorticist periodical *Blast!*) were thus anti-humanist and antidemocratic, driven to create new forms mostly because the old ones seemed irredeemably contaminated by the tradition. They saw themselves both as moderns and as defenders of a European high culture under attack by commercialism. So shallow was their social thought that they blamed the Jews, actually crucial to the creation of that culture, for its erosion. They also hated and feared the working class as brutal, vulgar, and mindless.

What the formalist avant-gardes of this period had in common, then, was an awareness that they faced a radically new social reality that the old forms could not contain. They struggled to define themselves in relation to the two major forces of the epoch that, as in Russia, often turned out to be inextricably intertwined—capitalist modernization and the working-class movement.

The only formalist avant-garde in American poetry today is the "language-centered writers" or language poets. Capitalizing on the stagnation and intellectual incoherence of American poetry since the mid-seventies, the language poets have constituted themselves as a rival hegemony to the neo-academic style that currently rules the universities and major publishing houses. They base their activity on the work of various "post-structuralist" thinkers, notably Jacques Derrida and Julia Kristeva. These thinkers have gone beyond the structural linguistics and semiology of Saussure and his successors to imply that language really refers only to itself, since behind the signifier "dog" is not the pure idea of a dog—let alone a real dog—but only more signifiers that define "dogness" and that in turn are defined by still other signifers, and so on. Hence, conclude the language poets, there is no thought outside language, no possible perception that is not conditioned by the dominant discourse (a conclusion already latent in structuralism). Since this discourse is the product of capitalist society, no truly radical break with this society is conceivable—by anybody—until its discourse has been "deconstructed."

Two further conclusions follow from this argument. According to the language poets, conformist perceptions and habits are rooted not merely in vocabulary but in syntax, grammar, and conventional narrative or expository structure. Thus, poetry which is narrative or descriptive is reactionary and dishonest; using language in these conventional ways helps reproduce the illusion that it is "transparent," i.e., that it has a one-to-one relationship to reality, when in fact it only refers to itself. Moreover, since most writing is produced by "professionals" (which the language poets proudly proclaim themselves to be), narrative, descriptive or argumentative poetry is "totalitarian"; it unilaterally imposes meaning on the nonprofessional reader.

In response to this ideology, the language poets have produced two tightly connected bodies of work. One of these is a poetry that is deliberately fragmentary and flat, that deliberately leads the reader nowhere—except, presumably, to admiration at the erudition of the authors, who drop names, quotations, and references constantly. This flatness and fragmentation ostensibly aim to let the reader collaborate "democratically" in creating the meaning of the text. The other part of the group *oeuvre* is an enormous mass of theoretical essays and "talks" that elaborate, usually in very gnarled prose mingled with the most naively candid self-promotion, the rationale for the poetry. Needless to say, this endless exegesis gives the lie to the "democratic" and demystifying claims made for the "poetry"; if it's really so open-ended, why spend so much time explaining its sources and minutely analyzing the process of its composition? In fact, "language poetry" is read by even fewer people than other modern poetry. Its populist pretensions are absurd.

Moreover, "language" ideology is founded on profound misconceptions about language itself. First of all, while language does play a vital role in shaping people's experience of the world, it's by no means the only or the most important factor. Arguably no less central, for instance, are the prelinguistic experiences of early infancy analyzed by Freud, and the constant bombardment of nonverbal images via TV, billboards, and so forth. Perhaps most central of all is the way experience and identity are structured by our everyday routines—by the *material facts* of an individual job done primarily to earn money, of individual purchase of the means of life and leisure, of privatized living and consumption arrangements. This centrality explains both why workers are socially passive and isolated most of the time—and why they are capable, in mass strikes and insurrections, of forming new kinds of social relationships with blinding speed. Work-for-pay-for-consumption is a highly articulated mechanism that can easily fall apart once its linchpin, the work routine, is broken collectively.

This leads me to the other fatal flaw in language ideology, which is its assumption that the existing discourse is more or less unilaterally imposed by authorities of various kinds—including "professional writers." It's a radical truism, of course, that we inherit the language we use from the society we're

born into, and that the language is strongly shaped by the "ideas of the ruling class." On the other hand, a moment's examination of contemporary American idiom shows that it's also shaped continuously from below—notably by "marginal" groups such as 'sixties hippies, gays and (especially) Blacks, all of whom have translated the discomforts of their relationship to mainstream society into brilliantly inventive slang. Moreover, meaning is reshaped and negotiated at a more microscopic level in every interaction: transformed via intonation, gesture, and shared frames of reference in ways happily impossible to control.

•

Some other poetic tendencies, notably Surrealism, have made a more intriguing claim for political effectiveness. This claim might be summarized as the idea that the poetic experience—the effect generated in the reader/listener by true poetry—is itself subversive and liberating.

This idea is an important point of convergence between formalist and non-formalist modernism. The Russian Formalists claimed that the poetic effect was a "defamiliarization" of language within the work; this was achieved by "foregrounding" language itself through the "devices" of metaphor, image, rhythm, sound, and so forth. While the Formalists themselves drew no political conclusions from this line of thought, it is not hard to do so. If poetry defamiliarizes language, might it not also call into question familiar assumptions about the existing social order? In his plays, Bertolt Brecht employed "alienation effects" whereby the audience would be made to question the naturalness of the all-too-typical characters and events portrayed; his poems likewise turn banal phrases inside out for inspection by the reader. For their part, the Surrealists hoped to produce a generalized "revelation" by encouraging ordinary people to record their dreams and practice automatic writing, so as to confront them with the radicality of their own deeper desires.

Such sweeping ambitions for poetic writing were clearly misplaced. At the moment when poetic writing became widely available through mass literacy and cheap printing techniques, it was marginalized in popular consciousness by lowest-common-denominator commercial mass culture, which exploited the power of the new media with ruthless efficiency. Only very specific social conditions, as I have suggested, seem somewhat to reverse this marginalization.

Still, the notion that poetry is inherently subversive goes back at least to Blake, who wrote in *The Marriage of Heaven and Hell* that Milton was "a true poet, and of the Devil's party without knowing it." Plato, who would have banned poets from the ideal society depicted in his *Republic,* clearly concurred. Other authoritarians throughout modern history have also demonstrated their agreement by jailing, torturing, murdering, and otherwise silencing poets whose work often has little ostensible political content.

In his essay "The Politics of Poetry," Hans Magnus Enzensburger argues that authoritarians hate poetry—and that poetry subverts authoritarian societies—because it *tells the truth about subjective experience;* it introduces ambiguity, doubt, nameless desires and fears, unauthorized perceptions. In this way it interrupts "the speechless howl of applause" that authority constantly attempts to elicit from its subjects. Enzensburger comes very close to concluding that the only possible political poetry is one of irony and protest, since poetry can't affirm any social power such as a leader, a party, or a state. That is certainly the view taken by Eastern European writers such as Zbigniew Herbert and Milan Kundera, who have witnessed at first hand the disastrous results of some poets' naive enthusiasm for Stalinist "revolutions."

Such pessimism is obviously conditioned by a fear of any sort of collective emotion; yet libertarian revolts need collective emotion just as much as do authoritarian ones. In libertarian revolts, it becomes difficult to separate the political-agitational and strictly poetic aspects of poems. Miguel Hernandez's tenderly personal "Lullaby of the Onion," written to his baby son while he was dying in one of Franco's prisons in 1940, became a powerful political statement when read aloud at a meeting of Madrid Univesity students thirty-five years later, when Franco himself was on his deathbed. The effect of revelation through the concentration of language devices like metaphor, proper to good poems, merges with the revelation of shared passion and purpose that is the aim of good political speech.

This politicized reawakening of a poem can happen because the poetry in a poem is always only a *potential* released through relationship to a particular reader at a particular moment in the reader's life and in history. Obviously, some poems have more of this potential than others. That is the difference between good and bad poems. But the poetry in some poems comes to life as they are read, sometimes lying dormant for decades or even centuries until the right connection is made.

What is this poetry, this potential? It is created in poetic language by means of image, metaphor, metonymy, rhythm and sound; these devices, as the Formalists pointed out, "foreground" language itself. Since most perception in adults is mediated through language, this has the effect of defamiliarizing and thereby renewing one's experience of the world. I would add to this analysis the Surrealist view of language as the "royal road" to one's unconscious life, to the raw associative and synthetic power of the imagination driven by desire. (Some psychoanalysts have suggested that the unconscious is organized like a language, and it has been demonstrated that dreams involve elaborate chains of puns and word associations.)

●

Poetry, then, is a quality of experience induced by specific conditions.

One of these is poetic writing. Are there others? The Romantic tradition down through the Surrealists, certainly, affirms that there are. They include poetic paintings (Kaspar David Friedrich, Gericault, Max Ernst), poetic musical works (*The Magic Flute,* Richard Strauss, Bartok), poetic films (*Zero for Conduct, Vertigo, The Color of Pomegranates),* poetic types of landscape (mountains, heathlands, rocky shores), poetic times of day (dawn, dusk, moonlit nights), and poetic modes of human relation (sexual love, chance encounter between strangers, intellectual friendship). That this is largely a catalog of cliches only testifies to the nearly universal power of the experiences from which the cliches derive. Any number of pictorial rocky shores or moonlit forest nights, for instance, does little to reduce the impact of these situations in reality. The question remains: what makes them poetic? Or, more precisely, what do we mean when we say they're poetic?

I won't attempt a definitive answer; but I suspect that Shelley was onto something in his *Defense of Poetry* when he wrote of the imagination as a kind of meta-faculty, as the synthesizing power of the mind that coordinates input from its other functions (feeling, intellect, sensation, intuition) to assemble a meaningful experience of the world. If this is so, then poetic experiences are ones in which the imagination, stimulated by the defamiliarizing effect of a poem, a work of art, or a real situation, is operating at a heightened level. This further implies that the mind's other faculties are working together in an unusually harmonious and effective way, rather as the coherence of frequency imparted to a beam of light by a laser greatly enhances the beam's range and power. In this state, dramatic reorganizations of individual experience are common, giving the sense that, as Yeats put it, "all is changed, changed utterly."

These words are from the refrain of Yeats's poem "Easter 1916," which brilliantly evokes the mood of the ill-fated Easter Rising against British rule in Ireland. A popular insurrection, to paraphrase Engels, is surely the most defamiliarizing thing there is. The whole texture of everyday life is transformed as the routines that constituted it are shattered. The individual finds herself in a suddenly altered and open-ended relationship to the whole world: to fellow workers, to strangers in the streets, to buildings and vehicles and machines, to the merchandise that may now be distributed gratis, to space and time. The imagination is summoned to the fore as possibilities become apparently limitless, as the individual is called on to help shape new ways of organizing social life, as previously unsuspected passions and previously inconceivable ideas flood her spirit. Yeats concludes his refrain: "a terrible beauty is born." This beauty, I believe, is poetry.

Yet the poetic quality of insurrections (and of lesser upheavals like strikes "from below," riots, and even some demonstrations) is both more overwhelming and less durable than the effect of genuine poetic language. Revolts, after all, involve often horrifying violence, severe discomfort and boredom as well as exhilaration, creative passion, and hallucinatory beauty. A true poem, while infinitely weaker in its effect on the individual life and imagination, provides the experience in an uninterrupted form, which can be renewed at one's convenience. Moreover, there are certain fields of awareness, fundamentally solitary and nonverbal, that poems or other works of art can summon and that the noisy, accelerated, preeminently social quality of revolt leaves little room for.

Beyond poems, beyond revolt, is a more poetic daily existence possible? The Situationists, and before them the Surrealists, called for a poetic transformation of life, for Lautreamont's "poetry made by all, not by one." Both groups understood that for this to be possible, the burden of forced, alienated labor—of toil, as William Morris called it—must be lifted from the backs of ordinary people. Morris and the Situationists pointed out that much work is useful only to business or the state, and that most of the remaining necessary tasks could be drastically reorganized, distributed among many more people, or mechanized out of existence. In a genuine social revolution, then, the creativity of millions would be engaged in this enormous reinvention of production, distribution, communications, architecture, and settlement patterns. Yet once the insurrectionary phase was past, there would still be more time than ever before for wandering, daydreaming, inquiring, playing, making love or making poems. Poetry would also permeate necessary work to a much greater degree once this work was controlled and designed by those who performed it. Of course, the necessity of standardized components in any sophisticated mechanical or electronic goods would limit creativity here, just as ecological considerations would constrain mechanization. But part of any creative endeavor is finding ways around such obstacles.

More generally, I find it impossible to imagine a world, however free, without occasional boredom, discomfort, depression, or lowered sensitivity. A successful social revolution would not eliminate these "prosaic" aspects of life, any more than it would eliminate aging and dying; it would, rather, subordinate them to the poetic ones.

IAIN BOAL:

There is political poetry that is awaiting its hour. Usually, it's true, "poetry makes nothing happen"; but this is not because it belongs to some transcendent realm or defies commodification, as Auden wished, but because the vast bulk of cultural production is kitsch—that is, it reproduces the official consciousness of the epoch. Political poetry, given the right conditions, mobilizes by crystallizing tangible but as yet unexpressed experience.

This crystallizing can produce the shock of recognition, can speak for us. And a poem can produce a new and potent symbolism by restructuring our perception. By choosing a semantic field that carries heavy cultural freight, there is the seldom-realized possibility of powerful agitational effects. For example, Tom Paulin's "The Book of Juniper" attempts a new cultural symbolism out of the ordinary experience of Irish landscape and the "green springy resistance" of the juniper. "For no one knows / if nature allowed it / to grow tall / what proud grace / the juniper tree might show / that flared, once, like fire / along the hills. On this coast / it is the only / tree of freedom / to be found ... now dream / of that sweet / equal republic / where the juniper / talks to the oak, / the thistle, / the bandaged elm, / and the jolly jolly chestnut."

Here is one Celtic reader agitated. But so what? Agreed. Nevertheless, its *potential* effect remains. The reason for that is language, which is always an arena of struggle—over definitions, meanings, and terms of reference. Poets are supposed to be especially implicated in this struggle, and Plato's banning of poets from the ideal Republic is often wheeled on as evidence. Still, Plato's situation and our own are laughably dissimilar.

Of prime importance is the fact that in the US there is no public space to speak of—space is what is left over from highway and shopping mall construction. Space is a residual category, weaving between speculators' lots. In this public space that isn't, there is no public discourse. In the Athens of Plato's time there were sacred spaces for democratic oral culture; large state resources were dedicated to theatrical events where poetry became the dominant medium for crystallizing the community's representations of its hopes, anxieties, conflicts—the amphitheater of ideological struggle, as it were. Serious agitation and the erotic excitement of public discourse: citizens had vast chunks of Homer, lyric, and drama by rote, and poetry was constantly cited as warrant for social and political practices.

●

The collapse of aristocratic patronage threw artists and writers into the capitalist markets. Bohemia and the avant-gardes were a response to this development, but there was no way out of *some* relationship with the system. The various vanguards marched in different political directions, from anarchism to fascism; but whatever their political tendency, they all aimed at making over the language or vocabulary of their art. The inadequacy of language in relation to felt experience is surely a real phenomenon, more or less acute depending on the historical moment.

The sources of the new language are various: Rimbaud invoked *dérangement,* the Dadaists relied on chance, the Surrealists turned to the unconscious. On the formalist side, the Russian Futurists and their Formalist boosters looked to linguistics for inspiration and justification of their art, as do their heirs—the Language poets, the rearguard of the new.

The Futurists/Formalists and the Language poets are linked by the figure of Roman Jakobson. Jakobson, who coined the term structuralism in the late twenties, claims that the new linguistics drew inspiration from Cubist art, which was concerned with the relationship *between* objects, with the syntax of form. Connect the dots: Jakobson began among the Muscovite artistic bohemians and ended up as a professor at MIT, where Noam Chomsky was his protégé. Later, one of Chomsky's disciples was George Lakoff, who has become a theoretician of the Language poets.

The move to formalism in linguistics was at first a very powerful technique. But in attempting to become "scientific," linguists in the thirties in North America fetishized form and became paranoid about meaning, which was, for positivists, slippery and unmeasurable. (This development parallels the rise of behaviorism and work on rats.) The formalist legacy is still with us: Chomsky believes that syntax—pure form—is the engine of language. Lakoff, who began by researching irregularity in syntax, revolted and now works on metaphor. But even linguists who have apparently abandoned the exclusive focus on syntax still tend to be formalists: semantics is concerned with objects that are formal, Platonic, ideal, far above the amphitheater of the struggle over reference.

JAMES BROOK:

"Politics": the public life of people, or the alienated realm of governmental and quasi-governmental activities? Most political poetry is concerned with the latter.

Two types of political poetry virtually monopolize the field of propaganda-by-verse, if advertising and political speeches are excluded from consideration: First, there's the poetry written by sympathizers with foreign or minority struggles for "independence." This poetry typically mixes sincere expressions of concern and solidarity with narcissistic self-absorption and sentimentality, as in Carolyn Forché's writing about El Salvador. Second, there's the poetry written by representatives of "national liberation" organizations. Usually written in the voice of a mythologized "People" but from the standpoint of militant bureaucrat, this poetry is hortatory and full of "therapeutic" national and class pride. The works of the talented Stalinist Pablo Neruda and Ernesto Cardenal demonstrate the rhetorical strengths of this tendency, while Roque Dalton's oeuvre constitutes its unintentional parody.

Paeans to hazy socialist dawns, mock epics celebrating papier-maché heroes, dilute romanticism combined with outmoded, conventional realism: How can such boring appeals to "struggle" and "sacrifice" for the State have inspirational effect? Unfortunately, national anthems continue to stir the souls of people who would be better off without the governments that "lead" them.

A third kind of political poetry, written by such poets as Mayakovsky, Brecht, Victor Serge, and Kenneth Rexroth (neither revolutionary tourists nor party hacks), attempts to extend subjectivity to public life and publicize private life in a nonreductive way, criticizing the spectrum of alienation, from "love" to "politics."

But are many people "influenced" or "radicalized" by poems about politics? Given that there is, first of all, only a miniscule audience for poetry in the United States today and, secondly, that there is no popular oppositional movement that could form a larger audience, it seems a joke to speak of the agitational effect of engagé verse. And is that what poetry is "for"?

•

Poets of the formalist avant-gardes believed that by means of dissociation and recombination of linguistic elements normal, "constraining" syntax would be broken down and words would be "set free." When taken to its logical conclusion by Russian Futurists like Khlebnikov, this poetry ended up excluding meaning and focusing on the supposedly liberatory effects of perceiving literary/linguistic devices "in themselves." Brecht, who used the formal innovations of the avant-garde, retained a grasp on content, retained a sense of purposeful communication that set his work apart from both the solipsistic modernist poets and the "socialist" poets who versified the party line.

Whereas Brecht and the Surrealists—revolutionary artists who were in some respects anti-avant-garde—wanted to "change life" and "transform the world," the formalist avant-gardes generally had less grand ambitions: perhaps a different perception of art and an aestheticization of "life" but not necessarily a "transformation" in the Marxist/Surrealist sense of the word.

Ridiculous as it may seem this late in the century, the Language Poets present themselves as an avant-garde. Like the Russian Formalists before them, the Language Poets hold to a strict separation of form and content (while subsuming content under form), and they denigrate as "romantic" works that point to any "signified" or "referent"; that is, works that communicate. This stance, like so much other "postmodernist" posturing, was rendered indefensible over half a century ago by Bakhtin/Medvedev's *The Formal Method in Literary Scholarship* (1928). But these ambitious academics persist in believing that their "scandalous" attack on meaning, the subject, syntax, content, and other nonlinguistic components of literature aligns them with a radical critique of capitalism.

Life is elsewhere: the Language Poets' emphasis on the subjectivist, private consumption of writing and the pseudo-objectivity of its production shows how close they are to mainstream commercial culture—their work is as essentially meaningless and hedonistic as that of Laurie Anderson, Philip Glass, The Talking Heads, and American politics, whose best song-and-dance is called "Ronald Reagan."

Consider: Like Language Poetry, Reagan has no "I," and his image is an extremely "nonreferential" "text" left "open" to each reader's solitary interpretation. The reader—isolated en masse—is urged to "participate" in Reagan's illusory destruction of "hierarchy," while leaving real hierarchical structures intact. Every Reagan speech "lays bare its devices" and "defamiliarizes" reality until it's unrecognizable. And Reagan, the voice of a committee, is a function of language, an intersection, an interface without "subjectivity." Finally, though Reagan might have an authoritarian personality (like Barrett Watten), he is not an "author" (again like Barrett Watten).

●

Octavio Paz wrote in *The Bow and the Lyre*: "There is . . . poetry without poems; landscapes, persons, and events are often poetic: they are poetry without being poems. Now, when poetry is given as a condensation of chance or when it is a crystallization of powers and circumstances alien to the poet's creative will, we are in the presence of the poetic. When—active or passive, awake or sleeping—the poet is the wire that conducts and transforms the poetic current, we face something radically different: a work . . . . The poetic is poetry in an amorphous state; the poem is creation, poetry standing erect."

But this begs the question whether the poem is to be considered a privi-

Roland Topor

leged site for poetry, a question I think answered by the Situationist, Raoul Vaneigem in *The Revolution of Everyday Life:* "'What is poetry?' ask the aesthetes. And we may as well give them the obvious answer right away: poetry rarely involves poems these days . . . . At best, the artist's creativity is imprisoned, cloistered, within an unfinished *oeuvre,* awaiting the day when it will have the last word . . . ."

What does this perspective mean for a poet writing now? While the Surrealists, after their early heroic period, wanted to continue producing in (and speculating in) the old artistic forms as they awaited the ever-postponed social revolution, the Situationists gradually abandoned the production of art as such and turned their attention to the construction of situations that would open the way for a libertarian revolution based on workers councils. Art came to mean everything for the Surrealists and nothing for the Situationists.

The Situationists saw how art became distorted by the market and by its function in the spectacle as well as how it had become outclassed technically by the mass media. As a remedy, they elaborated the theory and use of "detournement"—the appropriation and derisive reinvestment of cultural artifacts—a procedure suggested to them by Lautréamont's *Poésies.* That this was a superior new means for revolutionary propaganda was testified to by the success of Situationist slogans and methods in the near-revolution of May '68 and in the infiltration of their ideas *as ideology* (revolutionary ideas minus revolutionary practice) into the punk scene and the universities a decade later.

But as a poet who appreciates the practical insufficiencies of Surrealism as well as the value of Situationist critique and methods, I am still reluctant to give up poetry writing in favor of detournement and other negative propaganda techniques; these practices are *not satisfying,* especially during reactionary times. I feel, above all, the lack of some measure of self-realization that is not ironized, made strange, alienated, put in quotes.

When then is a poet who is also a revolutionary—and *not* a neo-Bolshevik politico—to do? It seems foolish to write poems that no one will read. If the present seems to have no use for poems, the future is notoriously unreliable. Perhaps a change of genre is in order—to gain audience if not "influence" (pet fantasy of unacknowledged legislators).

To be reexamined: the cases of Mayakovsky and the Bolshevik coup/ revolution, Péret and the Spanish Revolution, Brecht and the triumph of Nazism and Stalinism.

TOM CLARK:

The question arises, is there, in this contemporary yupped-up, laser-equipped, top-loaded, super-administered Star Wars balloon payment techno beep-creep gourmet-consumer-video-terminal society, any place or function for art, and if so, what?

Of course the relation of art to politics has always been one of those classic Venus flytrap subjects, enticing well-meaning suckers into sticky wickets. Escape routes like "commitment," "propaganda," and "the dialectic" have been shown to be shortcuts to nowhere—imponderables that have about as much to do with art as acronyms do with language.

Knowing this, it's only with a sad conflicted sigh of incipient oblivion that one dares to stare the question in the eye. But then again one remembers that the folly of all political-aesthetic reflection is also its great charm and appeal. The beauty of any truly hopeless endeavor is that at least you can be sure there won't be any spin-off merchandising. And indeed, to slightly mutate the phrase Artaud applied to Van Gogh, the true artist in our time is a person suicided by late capitalist society, adrift on a polystyrene air mattress in a sea of false consciousness and last-ditch human greed and confusion and grinning orthodontists jogging across reconstructed urban wastes in Reeboks. And then there's the language school. The language school is the logical heir to Carlos Castaneda in the endless dialectic (that word again) of period commodity art. Using appropriate semio-structuralist jargon, the language school distills the Yuppie Way of Knowledge into conveniently assimilable socio-aesthetic programs reflecting a quotient of mutual admiration and wishful thinking that outdoes the tower builders of Babel for sheer self-deception yet remains broadly attractive in ways intelligible to any shepherd—i.e., the bell tinkles, the sheep come. On the other hand, it remains true that the "answer" is not to simply write poems or paint pictures with "messages" or "about politics" (workers, revolutions, etc.). It's superficial to assume that subject matter limits the political in art. A poem about a proletarian or a rebellion is no more "relevant" than a poem about a geranium or a rainbow. The goal of "political relevance" can be forced on art only in the way a heavy load is forced on a pack animal. Beasts of burden = agitprop art works. As Theodor Adorno pointed out, Kafka, without addressing monopoly capitalism directly, laid bare the basic inhumanity of the modern administered world, and did so more powerfully and uncompromisingly than if he had written novels about corruption in multinational corporations. W. C. Williams is a more "political" poet in his poems about the chicken and the rain water or the plums in the icebox than in the parabolic "political" poem "The Yachts." Real art resists death, the granddaddy of all domination, and in doing so allies itself with life, the bio-mass, and the great World

Breath of Creation, or what's left of it.

Expression figures prominently here. Expression is the negative of suffering. Art is intrinsically pro-life and anti-society. It is *for itself,* not for me or you or the revolution. It resists domination and repression and bossing-around of all kinds. It especially resists the kind of aesthetic codification which would turn it into a pack horse (beast of burden) for some agenda or other. Art is not a placard or a sandwich board bearing the stencilled lettering of a union, an initiative, or anything else. It is, rather, utopian and political in the most radical of ways. To the degree that a society totally free of repression is from any historical perspective an absolute contradiction in terms, art, whose tendency is to remain free, opposes and resists all existing social forms. Artistic autonomy and social anarchy go hand in hand. Art has (as it were) a will of its own. Its inner coherence (or lack of same) determines its truth (or lack of same). As for the avant-garde, it's been a halfway house for fakers for so long one can no longer think about it without conjuring up ridiculously comical associations of aging youth, tenured academics in jogging shorts. If anything's going to save us from the current blitzkrieg of silliness it certainly won't be *THAT!*

Ovid: The True Metamorphoses

ALBERTO SAVINO

Translated from the French by James Brook

Poets do live in their works but only rarely do they live on in their own bodies. Corporeal survival is the prerogative of men having nothing to do with poetry: Frederick Barbarossa survived in his own body—as he lies next to his faithful swordfish, he awaits the end of his long nap so that they may once again cross swords. Michel de Notre Dame survives in his tomb with paper, pen, and ink within arm's reach; but unlike Barbarossa, who sleeps lying down, Nostradamus sleeps standing up, like a thoroughbred horse. Garibaldi still lives for the dwellers on the shore of the Sea of Azov who day after day expect him, the harbinger of freedom and everything good. Oscar Wilde lives in the sordid districts of Paris, flabby and pale like a drowned man, dead enough as a poet but still living in his obscene, pitiful body, a participant in black masses. But no one could rival Publius Ovidius Naso who, even though a poet, lives on in the flesh and prowls day and night in the area near Sulmona, his native town.

It was just a few months ago that Timoleon and I arrived at the Fountain of Love near Sulmona and asked for news of Ovid from two young men watering their horses—we learned that although they did not know Ovid personally, we would find people in the nearby village of Marana who could give us precise information about him.

I had convinced Timoleon to follow me in my wanderings with the object of finding Ovid in places that he used to frequent and, according to credible evidence, that he now haunted, sometimes disguised as a devil and sometimes as a vision of love.

During his August 1883 trip to Sulmona, Paul Parzanese wrote that everyone in the area spoke of Ovid and that "heaven and earth also spoke of him, in an amorous light." I too stopped at Sulmona, and with a trap-setter's patience I lay in ambush: first, by Ettore Ferrari's statue representing Ovid with stylus raised as he awaited inspiration, and then near a confectioner's shopwindow full of little baskets and ready-made wreaths with multicolored candies—I hoped that Ovid would come to this window like a lion to a stream, at night, to quench his thirst. Finally, I lurked at the entrance to the Santissima Annunziata where a statue of Ovid showed the poet wrapped in a cloak, with one foot resting on a book. Later on, I got back into Timoleon's car, and we drove off toward the Fountain of Love.

It was raining. Our little car splashed a passerby who shouted out: "Mannaggia Guiddie!"—for the inhabitants of Sulmona still swear by Ovid's name, just as in Galicia they still swear by the name of Titus ("Titz hurrah!"), in whose reign Solomon's temple was built.

We finally came to the village of Marana. We asked an old man sitting on his doorstep and smoking a pipe whether he had seen Ovid.

"Yes," he replied. "A few minutes ago it was coming down in buckets and there was so much lightning you would've sworn it was daytime. I was walking along by myself when all of a sudden I heard the sound of a carriage and horses galloping up. I turned around to look, but the carriage went by quick as an arrow. I looked after it in the distance and saw that the horses were made of fire."

Timoleon asked him whether the rumors circulating in the area about Ovid's survival weren't nonsense, fruits of the fertile imagination of the inhabitants of Sulmona, who were too easily influenced by the Dantesque setting of the mountain and valleys surrounding the town. But the old man heartily denied that such was the case, and with a clarity of thought and aptness of expression that demonstrated his grasp of ancient wisdom, he said:

"Officially, Ovid died in Tomis in 17 A.D., and that marked the beginning of his real transformations, of which his book *The Metamorphoses* was only the introductory essay. First, Ovid became a necromancer and went to live on Mt. Morrona, a nearby mountain that only the darkness prevents our seeing. On the slopes of Mt. Morrona there can be found—arranged on superimposed planes— first, the Fountain of Love, where Ovid flirted with Augustus' daughter; second, the villa surrounded by gardens, where the poet still lives; and, last, the hermitage where Celestine V, the Pope who refused to reign, went to meditate. People came to see Ovid as a master in the art of love. Impotent lovers had recourse to him; and because Ovid knew the science that 'loosens and binds,' he roused the dormant love with a philtre of his own manufacture. Then, tired of necromancy, Ovid recognized his errors and became a Christian. He had always been a Christian in spirit, and he even left the memory of Christian virtue with the barbarian population in whose proximity he had lived out his bitter exile. The peasants there still recount how in those backward times a man of extraordinary virtues came to them from the banks of the Tiber. He had the mildness of a child and the kindness of a father.

"He would often speak or whisper in an undertone to himself. But when he addressed someone, it was as if honey or nectar flowed from his lips. The natives of the region also claimed that Ovid wrote some poems in Moldavian; unfortunately, no trace of them remains.

"Eugène Delacroix, in one of his frescoes in the Palais-Bourbon, depicted Ovid in a soft and languid attitude, surrounded by admiring, stupefied, tender Scythians who, not daring to approach his person, frantically compete in offering him magnificent gifts. Ovid was a great scholar. His works were innumerable. As he wrote, his pen raced across the page without hesitation, and he never dipped it in the inkwell. Ovid's wisdom came to him via his nose, and that's why he was called Naso. Our saying, 'a man with a good nose,' corresponds to the Latin tag, *emunctae naris*. Jean de Bounsignori, who lived around 1300 and was the author of *Allegorie ed Exposizioni della Metamorfosi*, explains that Ovid was called Naso because 'as it is through the nose that we smell the odor of everything, Ovid tried to sniff out and know everything to do with his century.'

"Now an official Christian, Ovid founded a school here where he instructed children in Christian doctrine and *The Book of Seven Trumps*. He wrote a book of Christian maxims and a collection of short fables. He passed on the light of his wisdom to St. Peter Celestine, with whom he conversed all night over the well at the Mt. Morrona hermitage. Nothing remains of the many works of this 'continued' Ovid. At the beginning of the nineteenth century, a notable of Sulmona was still in possession of one of Ovid's books, but one of Napoleon's generals who happened by his house wanted to read the book and forced the man to lend it out. The next morning the general took off for France with the book, which enabled the French to make wonderful discoveries and inventions. Ovid's reputation reached as far as the King of Naples, who would not make laws without first consulting Ovid. His best friends were—and are—Cicero of Arpinum and Horace of Rome. Ovid was a monk, a preacher, and a saint. He belonged to the Church of Reims under the name St. Ovid the Martyr and was made the Bishop of Braga, in Portugal, where even today they sing in his honor:

Gaude Sacerdos Ovidii
Tu Bracharensis Pontifex.
Qui meruisti filia
Tot ad polos transmittere.

Day was beginning to break, and Timoleon expressed his desire to go see Ovid's villa. But the old man said that that was impossible.

"Ovid doesn't allow it. They don't even try to keep the road up, since Ovid would wreck it. A few years ago they erected a building for military target practice near the Fountain of Love, but Ovid destroyed it that very night. He wants to be left alone. How can you blame him?"

Despite this testimony, Timoleon was not convinced. "This survival through the centuries, tell me how you explain that."

"Poetry," said the old man. "The extraordinary power of poetry."

I had been looking off in the direction of Ovid's villa. When I turned back to face the old man, he was no longer there.

There was just a man-shaped glimmer.

But it vanished immediately.

Napoleon's Eye

When the blind Napoleon died, no one bothered to replace his glass eye, which remained on his nightstand, under two fingers of water in a bowl.

Napoleon was taken to the cemetery and put in the family vault.

That same evening, from the top of the nightstand, Napoleon's eye saw the conjugal bed profaned by the cavalier Stanislao, a lifelong friend and business associate. And he recognized on his widow's face that expression somewhere between ecstasy and anguish which he thought was his exclusive possession.

Then Napoleon's eye, gathering what small strength a glass eye can dispose of, leapt out of the water, sprang from the nightstand, traversed the room like a rocket, and, smashing all its hardness against an even tougher wall, fell to the floor in a crystalline rain.

The Bath of Venus

Venus is sleeping on the powderkeg. Watched over by giant gunners. There's a very big gun-carriage, then a smaller one, then another one smaller still; then there are many others of decreasing size and finally a minuscule gun-carriage. As Venus sleeps, her eye gleams in this tiny gun-carrier. Ash, gunpowder, and desolation everywhere. And up above, supported by enormous squares and colossal compasses, are the great stone cannons that have not spoken since the time of Francesco Ferruci.

But when the sky is clear and deep, Venus bathes in the azure and dries her coal-black feet on the clouds.

Venus is beautiful. That is a fact. Everyone says so. But you have to look at her from a distance. Up close, what can be seen, what can be "comprehended"? At most, one could sit on the nail of her big toe or, if it's raining, find shelter beneath her nostrils.

There was nothing tendentious about the gunner's invitation to me: "Come!" Then, in a different voice, he repeated: "Come!" Then a third time, in yet another voice, as if he were not just one but three individuals, he repeated: "Come!"

Yet this gunner knew that no one should watch Venus at her bath. The sight can kill.

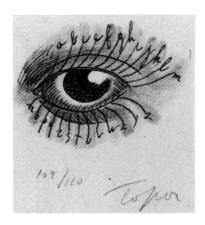

from

The Happiness Chronicles

BRIGITTE FONTAINE

Translated from the French by Barbara Szerlip

In the forests, in the red-embered towns beyond the sea, on the fragrant hills, lived a beautiful, warm and tawny beast called Happiness. She leapt everywhere, laughing in the night, dancing with fire, singing in all directions with the wolves.

This happened at no particular time because time, you see, is a mysterious thing.

This beast ate everything people gave it, she let herself be milked by them, she saw through them with her golden bough if they desired it, she made music with their veins and hair.

Yet there were those who hated her. Free and unfettered, she was out of step, she prevented them from holding sway. So one day they came with weapons and captured her, imprisoned her in a distant cage.

This happened in no particular place because countries, you know, are mysterious things.

So that people would not revolt, innumerable copies of the beast were made. So that people would be repelled, would no longer understand anything and would forget her, the copies were made badly. The false beast began to coo, play bridge, sell its sad enticements in the evening streets, sing operettas and wear pink ribbons like those one ties in the hair of little girls to prevent them from being what they really are: great, warm and tawny beasts.

People became bitter and sad, they snickered, stuffed themselves with cake, slapped themselves into a frenzy and thoroughly mocked the poodle called Happiness, the windbag known as Happiness. And then they forgot her, as was the plan (except for those few who'd been hospitalized).

Yet, reflected in the eyes of all the babies one can see the awful beast's shape, and it really seems as if her heat is in the process of melting the bars of her distant cage, there where the soldiers left her.

I met an old, old woman who'd lost all hope of seeing the beast return in her lifetime, "But," she told me, "I know she exists and after all that's what matters."

But that old woman will die soon and no longer need to lie.

• • •

So listen: Each being, at each second, carries in his watery depths an absolute and radiant happiness, regardless of what happens on the surface. (It's a pity that what's called "I" will never be aware or able to take advantage of it.) Some suspect its existence but don't want to get involved, as they've left a pot of milk to boil unattended on the stove.

And so the Carousel of the Great Conspiracy goes round and one must punch in and punch out of its machinery each day in order to verify one's existence.

We can assume that (with an exchange of ambassadors) the rebirth of this secret happiness would have the serious consequence of preventing people from killing each other.

Once having touched and recognized this absolute, radiant happiness, people will tolerate nothing less, they'll burst out laughing, sweeping off oppression with a strong but gentle backhand, finally rescuing the sun, captive these ten thousand years, these last fifteen minutes.

My name is Eel, I play bowls with the butterflies, I wipe the blood away with a magician's little blue silk handkerchief, I fasten the hoarfrost and sometimes do housework beneath the sea or in the eaves. Many things are happening in the eaves.

Good, says the impartial executioner, now we go to chop off our *own* heads.

Many things are happening in the rain-gutters. Commuters are requested not to make noise with their jaws when eating, not to laugh (it makes them ugly), never to stop trailing their own shadows: not to overflow, that's the law.

Sunday, the cigarette butts of Americans tumble down, still lit and large as the sea.

So the condemned one very sportingly says to the executioner, "Okay, let's go get our heads cut off."

Though I've told you my name is Mimi Pater Noster, it's a lie: the name's Carmen of the Flesh and I'm a mad scribbler.

Let those who don't suffer show themselves and I'll have them framed, 'cause my skipper liked to say there are kicks in the ass one has yet to enjoy. But I swear to you: there are *kisses* we've yet to enjoy! They flit around us between the houses and we don't see them.

There are pleasures we've yet to enjoy, rustling in the trees and in the body, and we don't see them.

There are countries whose citizens seem adept at entertaining birds.
Is that why we chain them up, bomb them, hang them by their feet?

Happiness breathes, sexes redden, eyelids gently alight, eyes stir with pleasure, men are returning from the war, the lawn receding on their heads.

On the tepid seats of afternoon, beautiful women scratch at their elastic-
cinched waists, drinks dream on the pale green tables. In the distance the river
naps; it's a good bet that summer's back. Flour trembles beneath the roofs, the
heaviness of the air prevents people from flying off and they rub against the
houses, muttering smiles.

Happiness breathes, a handsome serpent winds himself around a beam,
houses creak like beds and the barn, the barn where we unfold is an ardent
blaze.

I'm a unicorn in the midst of poppies, three green birds play in the sky, a
small gilded lake quivers, jewel-like, on my chest. Blood pulses through me like
water through a field, tracing its blue-gray tree. So then why has the war begun?

Barbara Szerlip

from

THE JAGUAR MYTHS

NANOS VALAORITIS

The Jaguars

for C.P. Kavafis

The jaguars are coming. Yes. They are coming, closing in on all sides. It is high time for the jaguars to arrive. They are all coming tomorrow. Very early in the morning before breakfast. Not just a few but many. Perhaps even thousands if not in the hundreds of thousands. They are coming for sure. That's what they said when they said they were coming. Tomorrow at three o'clock, to be more precise. The Jaguars. Many of them unspotted. Others just striped or black. Grey and pink Jaguars are unlikely to come. All kinds, all sizes, all shapes. Green yellowish eyes flashing in the night. Those who say they're not coming are fools. All the more fools are they, since they don't know what they're talking about. They have been sighted already not so far away from the town. I mean the city, the walled city. For we are still unattached to any form of civilization that's not ours. The everlasting bones chewed to death. Not a single letter still alive to tell the tale. The jaguars although somnolent are hungry for letters. And for music too beneath those stubborn skulls. It's been said they were overcome once by music. But that's long ago and now they don't appreciate music any more. The telegrams have all stated it clearly.

They are arriving in great numbers over rivers and forests, over steppes and tundras, over deserts and uninhabited areas. They are all converging here. What are they seeking? What reeking rotten flesh are they after? Some people say it's all right to give them parchments to eat. Others say they only demand salads, or honours. Only a few suspect the truth. The jaguars have to be fed with babies' flesh. No other will do. Is the sky electrical with semantic leaps? Is a man enamelled with memories unable to live long enough to see all his expectations fulfilled? The snarled events of his life will form quite a long list of retributions. But enough philosophizing. Will this man ever be? Since I wrote this the Jaguars have surrounded the city. They are trying to scale the walls with yelps and cries and growls. This is not going to be easy for them. Their leader Edward Jaguar is ready to parley. They demand a hostage. Contemplating the sea of Jaguars, some of us are beginning to have misgivings. What do they really want? As I was standing there looking from the highest pyramid of our town, it suddenly dawned on me. My ancestors, the priests, would have done nothing less than what I'm about to do. I now understand what all these Jaguars are about. This is going to be as difficult to describe as a Werner Herzog film. But I must do it to the end. The townspeople are imploring me to do it. A great calm has descended on the hoards of Jaguars as before a storm. The air is filled with electricity. The townsfolk are begging me on their knees. Then suddenly in a flash of lightning which illuminates the skies with thunderous claps from clouds of dust and steam, it occurs to me what the jaguars are really after. Why they have come such a long way over oceans and deserts. They want me. And more specifically my penis, or rather my phallus, if you wish. Why hadn't I thought of that before? We humans are so blind to other animal's desires. Yes my phallus of obsidian, symbol of power over generations of priest-kings, I repeat it without shame. I'm the object of their hunger. The decision was taken in an instant. From my neighbor the butcher I borrowed his elegantly carved electrical saw, bearing the head of a jaguar. Pardon me, Depardieu, for plagiarizing you, I muttered and I severed it with one quivering thrust and threw it to them. A great roar rose as they leaped up to catch it. The one who caught it was immediately devoured by the others, who devoured those who had devoured him, until in a carnage of mutual devoration not a single Jaguar was left. But no, I am mistaken, one was left. It was Edward Jaguar who had consumed them all. Together we contemplated the rising sun, the beast and myself. The sun rose over the field of the most majestic carnage in the history of the world. And as the odour of blood and flesh subsided, I looked at myself in the mirror that Edward Jaguar was holding up to me with his teeth. I was transforming into a woman. Breasts had grown where only tits had been, my long hair became shinier and curlier and black as ebony. My eyes sparkled, while the gathering crowds applauded wildly, not their saviour, but their saviouress, not their hero but their heroine: Myself. Rejuvenated from an old man to a young woman. While Edward Jaguar himself, already half-man, was holding my hand with carnivorous glee.

Beauty and the Beast

Edward Jaguar never became totally human. His animal self was still evident even after his animalectomy. The head remained jaguar-like. He spoke, but then he had always been able to speak. His body, although he walked upright, was more jaguar-like than human. His teeth and claws remained especially formidable. Sleeping with him was much closer to an act of bestiality. Even as a man I had never indulged in it. But now as a woman it was really strange to me. I have heard rumors of women making love with their animals. I had never really given it much thought. But now when confronted with these teeth, these claws that could spring at me any moment, I realized that the thrill of love could be mingled with the fear of death. This description is becoming too intimate for my taste. . . . Yet I cannot resist the details. That shiny black skin. That extraordinary tenderness and love of the animal. The feeding times when he will only take the raw flesh from my bare hands as delicately as a little pussycat. The purring. The growling whimpers when he makes love, to me. Our long walks in the outskirts of the jungle, and of course my fears that jealous humans will kill him. My jealousy in case he finds a female jaguar and runs away. How I would risk my life in the jungle looking for him. How I would wait for him faithfully to come back. How when he is angry with me he climbs trees and refuses to come down or take food for days. How I have sometimes locked him out of my room and he remains all night outside my door whimpering. This description is becoming too intimate for my taste. Yet I cannot resist indulging in it. I know I take risks and people may think dreadful things of me after they read this. But I have to be faithful to what I believe and honest with myself. Although honesty in the general sense is only a bourgeois value, a safeguard for merchants, a business ethic, yet honesty to oneself is the writer's prerogative. It is even an obligation, a duty, a pleasure. The thought has crossed my mind. A desire so terrible and obscure that I dread to utter it. I now have only one obsession left in my life. I want to become an animal. I want to be able to run freely with my beloved Edward, to climb trees without fear of falling. To hunt with him and eat raw flesh. Does that sound as terrible as all that? Have I not got the right to belong to any species I like? No question about it. When we went to the Jaguar-priest and asked him to perform the transformation, it was like getting married in the Church. We both stood before him and he asked me: "Will you take Edward to be your lawful wedded animal?" Blushing, I said Yes, with all the passion I could work up in my voice. He too growled his assent when the priest said, "Will you take Nan O to be your lawful wedded wife?" And we held paws, and kissed, with scrapy tongues. "All right," said the priest, "now run along, my children, and have fun..." And we ran off, I for the first time on all fours and smelling the odors of the forest, a real symphony of smells, as my nose became sensitive to them, and pricking up my ears at the slightest sound . . .

The Pale Population

ALYSSA ERDLEY

I have not myself what could be called a ruddy complexion, but I do have enough color in my face, at least, to tell that I'm alive. This was not the case with the new man at the office, the fellow they got to replace my last assistant.

Pale to an extreme, and provokingly thin, he hardly seemed a being of this, our world. He floated unevenly when he walked, as though on the verge of toppling over. Rarely did he utter a word, not even to me, but he completed his assignments adequately and I had nothing to complain of in his demeanor or general attitude.

With a sense of duty and natural generosity, I struggled to overcome, or at least to conceal, my dislike of the man, which was based only upon irrational and subjective impressions. Unfortunately for my efforts, the pale-faced assistant did nothing to reverse these most powerful impressions. Indeed, he did in every way increase my antipathy and confirm the justice of my prejudice. His personality, if one could claim he possessed one, seemed homeopathically linked to the chill vacuity of his features so that he seemed less like a human being than like a dense wall of cold and damp stuff. Soon his very presence oppressed me and I felt ill every day I had to come into the office and suffer it.

I would have gotten used to him in time, as one gets used to even the most intolerable things, if it were not for a remarkable coincidence. It was around the same time that this new man began to work at the office that I noticed a moving van parked one afternoon right in front of my apartment building. Naturally, I was mildly curious about the new tenant and I lingered about, hoping for a chance to catch sight of him.

My passive efforts were soon rewarded, as they usually are in such a small building, and a strange man swung onto the balcony corridor. I was struck dumb on the instant I saw his face. How could Fortune be so cruel—of a whole city of choices, that my detestable companion from the office should move into my very own apartment building.

But perverse fears had made me their victim, and a second glance assured my strained and vulnerable senses that I had been mistaken. The two men looked very similar to one another, it was true. Both were very tall and gaunt, and both had that stringy, gray hair that overshadowed that same sickly face, but there the resemblance ended; they were definitely not one and the same. Never-theless, and as unjust as it was, I conceived an instant dislike for my new neighbor, a sentiment solely based upon the false familiarity of those unaccept-able features. I made sure that I saw the man as infrequently as possible, but it was a very small building and I was often unsuccessful. Always, upon such unpleasant occasions, was I subject to the very same vague and uneasy appre-hensions already inspired in me by the pale young man at the office. I could no longer pretend he was someone whom I merely disliked, for my abhorrence of him, of his pallid face and those lifeless eyes, grew more and more with each passing day.

The other fellows in the office were in the habit of eating at a particularly roisterous cafeteria for lunch—it was a daily event and the source of much amusement and affable good cheer. But I was forced to discard this habitual pleasure, out of the necessity of avoiding my detestable co-worker, and I trudged instead to sad and squalid little lunchrooms, where I was certain not to meet a single member of my own profession. Despite the unhallowed atmosphere of these grim and murky places, the hour I spent in them was an hour of gratitude and blessed relief.

So certain I was of my safety, so serene in the success of my temporary escape, that it came as a blow, as a horrible shock, that day I saw him, through the dense smoke of the meanest hovel of them all, those flaccid, yet immutable features glowing palely separate from the swarthy complexions of the general crowd. My eyes could not be deceiving me, though the mist caused by my hatred gave the vision an unreal, shimmering quality of the fantastic.

Seized with violent revulsion, I sprang up from my seat, spurred on my pent up hatred, I strode across the room in order to confront the onerous crea-ture once and for all, when to my complete consternation and frustrated displea-sure, I discovered that this man wasn't the man from the office at all. I was entirely mistaken. But neither, as you might have conjectured, was he my equally detestable and similarly appointed neighbor. He was yet another young man, yet another despicable young man with those same unremarkable, yet intolerable features.

I hovered there in front of him, distressed to the last degree and shaking with rage. Some remnant of sanity, some shred of human decency bade me let the man be and return to my seat, but then perverse chance would have it that the fellow heard a noise, or was in some other way disturbed, so that he started and looked up in my direction. I was forced to meet those gray and emotionless eyes.

The blood rushed into my head. I was deafened and blinded. Propelled by some force more primitive and powerful than I can tell, I would have attacked—but my view of him was suddenly blocked, effectually, though inadvertently, by a waiter, who turned round to look at me ... he was nobody I'd ever seen before, and he was all three of them put together: the co-worker, the neighbor, and the man across the room. There was no end, no end at all, to the supply of these revolting, pale young men. He took a step toward me, for what purpose I know not, but I backed away horrified and groped my way dazedly for the door.

The fresh air hit me hard and there was a terrible glare from the clouds. It was dazzlingly bright on the street, as though a uniform wash of white had been laid over everything, draining colors and erasing shadows like some gargantuan application of bleach. Every face that passed me by looked so white, so very pale and sickly. But it wasn't just the pallor that I began to see.

First it was just one or two of them in the crowds pushing towards me, with those drooping eyelids and those stupid, hanging lips. Just one or two at first, and then, as I began to walk faster, as my throat began to tighten, there were small groups of them, three and four together, all with that gliding, lanky walk and that drab fall of hair across a promontoric forehead. Finally there were whole gangs of them loping listlessly up the street, entirely speechless and never glancing so much as left to right.

I began to run up the glaring pavement, my heart was racing, my lungs working forced and frantic; every face I saw was his face, every form that passed me by was his form. I must have been screaming, for there was a scorching pain in my throat and several men closed in upon me to subdue my wild actions. Pale, lanky men they were, with vapid faces; they circled round me and soundlessly approached. Hysterical with revulsion and convulsed by disbelief, I surrendered to them and gave myself up to the inevitable. I could feel their toneless arms clasp mine in limp embraces, feel their cold and clammy skins brush my own, and leave in their wake a tepid film of moisture. Their breaths blew into my face, shallow, damp, and uneven. I knew without looking that the contagion had spread, to myself.

Roland Topor

The Society Tiger

JEAN FERRY

Translated from the French by Ronald F. Sauer

Of all the music hall attractions stupidly dangerous to the public, as well as to their promoters, there is none to fill me with such supernatural horror as that old number known as the "society tiger." For those who have not seen it, as the younger generation is unaware of just what passed through the great music halls and into the twilight of the preceding era, I recall the particulars of that presentation. What puts me at a loss for words, what I cannot begin to explain, is the state of terrified panic and abject disgust into which this spectacle plunges me, as into some water at once suspect and atrociously cold. I should never even enter the theaters where this number, increasingly rare now anyway, figures as part of the program. Easier said than done. For reasons that I can shed no light upon, the "society tiger" is never announced, and I never expect it, or maybe I do, as if an obscure menace, formless but heavy, weighs upon the pleasure I take in music halls. If a sigh of relief lifts my heart after the last attraction has come to an end, I know only too well the fanfare and pomp which precede this number—always executed, as I have said, on the spur of the moment. And when the orchestra characteristically attacks that brassy waltz, I know what is going to happen next; a crushing weight takes hold of my breast, and a wire of fear winds between my teeth, like a sour, low dose of electricity. I ought to leave, but I no longer dare. Besides, nobody budges, nobody shares my anguish, and I know only this, that the beast is already en route. It seems like the arms of my seat will protect me, oh! but ever so feebly ...

To begin with, the theater is totally dark. Then a projector lights up in the foreground, and the beam of this derisive beacon illuminates an empty seat, more often than not, close to mine. Quite close. From there, the sweep of brightness seeks out an extremity of the stage, where a door opens into one of the wings, and as the horns of the orchestra dramatically attack the "Invitation to the Waltz," they appear.

The tamer is a poignantly beautiful redhead, rather weary. On both her arms float fans of black ostrich feathers, with which she at first hides the lower part of her face; only her immense green eyes remain to be seen over the dark

163

wave of undulating feathers. Her naked arms, now exposed in the light, glow iridescently—like a winter mist when a prism to the setting sun—and the effect of the low-cut, sleeveless evening dress that she wears is rather romantic as it clings to her, but also quite strange, full of heavy reflections and pools of profound blackness. And the dress has a fur trim, whose softness and fine aura are quite unbelievable. On top of it all, the eruption in cascades of that headful of flames, studded with gold stars. The total effect is oppressing and at once somewhat comical. But who would even think of laughing? The tamer, playing with a fan and using it to reveal those pure lips locked in an unmoving smile, moves forward, followed by the beam of projected light, toward the empty seat, arm in arm, so to speak, with the tiger.

The tiger walks humanly enough upon its hind legs; dressed up like a dandy, it looks elegantly refined, and its outfit is so perfectly tailored that it is difficult to distinguish, under the gray pants with spats, the flower-patterned vest, the blinding white dress shirt irreproachably pleated, the frockcoat fitted by the hand of a master, the animal's body. But the head with its horrible grin is there, the insane eyes rolling in their purple orbit, the furious hackling of its whiskers, and the fangs that at times glisten under lips curling back! The tiger advances, very stiff, a gray hat of high color in the hollow of his left arm. The tamer moves forward with measured steps, and if her loins tighten at times, if her bare arm contracts, revealing unforeseen muscles beneath the tawny velvet of skin, it is because with violent though disguised effort, she has just checked her cavalier who was about to fall forward.

And so they arrive at the door of their box seats which the tiger holds open with his paw, standing aside, this society tiger, so that his lady might pass. And when she has entered and sat down, after she has carelessly posed her elbows on the faded plush velvet, the tiger drops down beside her into a seat. At this point the audience usually breaks into complacent applause. And I, I just look at the tiger, and such is my longing to be somewhere else, I could cry. The tamer loftily acknowledges the room, with a nod of that headful of flaming locks. Then the tiger begins his labors, manipulating the accessories set before him for that purpose. He picks up a lorgnette and pretends to examine the audience with it, he opens a box of chocolates and makes a show of offering one to his neighbor. He takes out a perfumed silk handkerchief and feigns indulging a whiff of it. He pretends, to the crackling hilarity of people here and there, to consult the program. Then he waxes gallant, and leaning toward the tamer, affects to whisper some declaration in her ear. He responds as though offended and, between the pale satin of her beautiful cheek and the harrowing stenchful snout of the beast, she coquettishly situates the frail screen of feathers. To top it off, the tiger makes show of a heartfelt despair, wiping his eyes with the back of his furry paw. And all during this lugubrious pantomime, my heart bangs like a wild bird in the confines of my rib cage, for I, and only I, know that this circus of bad taste is sustained by a miraculous act of the will, as they say, that all of it horribly hangs by a thread and that some little nothing could make that thread snap. What would happen if, in the box beside the tiger, the little guy with the looks of a mild mannered employee, the little guy with the pale complexion and tired eyes, for one moment lost his concentration? For it is he who is the actual tamer, the redhead is just a decoy, a prop, and everything depends on him; it is he who makes of the tiger a marionette, a thing more surely bound than were it so by cables of steel.

But if this little man should suddenly start thinking of other things? If he dropped dead? Nobody doubts the possible danger, that moment by moment, is real. And I, who know it, can just imagine, just imagine, but no! it is better not to think about it, think what this woman with her fur trim would look like if … Better to think about how it all ends, which always reassures the public and sends them into ecstasies. The tamer asks if someone in the audience would care to entrust her with a child. Who could refuse anything to such a suave person? There is always someone unconscious enough to deliver their little darling right into the hands waiting in the maniacal box, and the tiger gently rocks it in the hollow of its paws, looking down at the little morsel with its alcoholic eyes. To the sound of thunderous applause, the lights come on, and the babe is returned to its rightful owner, and the two partners bow before withdrawing along the same path they had come.

As soon as they are gone for good, returning no more for additional bows, the orchestra knocks out its brassiest numbers. Shortly thereafter, the little guy begins to wilt and you can see him wipe his brow. The orchestra cranks it up some more, in order to drown out the roars of the tiger, restored to himself now in his cage. And he howls like hell, rolling about to tear off his fine, tailored suit that has to be remade for each new performance. These are the vociferations that burst from tragedy, the execrations of a desperate rage, and the clamoring racket of its furious boundings as it rattles the limits of its cage. On the other side of which the false tamer now hurries to change, so as not to miss the last metro. The little guy awaits her near the station, at a cafe named the Never Never.

The raging storm that the tiger unleashes might make a rather unpleasant impression upon the public, even at a distance. And for this reason the orchestra still gives it their all, pumping up the overture of "Fidelio," and why the stage manager in the wings hastens the cycling comedians on stage.

I despise this number, this "society tiger," and will never understand why the public eats it up as it does.

Charles Henri Ford

from

THE MINOTAUR SUTRA

What's beginning
Nothing the air is filled
With a poison of color

●

Green light on the
Gladiola leaves light you are
Green love you are mean

●

I showed him what I
Thought were worm eggs
Okra seeds he said

●

Lichen algae and
Fungi mystical masonry
Proliferates

●

My life is the morning
The morning goes I go
Until tomorrow

●

Palms stuck behind the
Hollow head interlocked hands
Of a ruined tree

●

Nostalgia is
An obvious blossom which
Opens its secrets

●

Flower of odorless
Beauty form may be
Conscious but not imposed

●

Blue hills blue hills of
Clouds a kite caught in a tree
Loses its color

●

Amorphous chance is
Only what you make it the
Leaves speak as they fall

Abd al-Hayy Moore

from

TALE OF THE GARDEN

1

Leaf over underleaf, a positive power,
orchid-like formations dripping with water-beads,
tiger-lily laughter of lollygagging stamens,
    wide petals drawn back like lips expressing joy
to speak in chorus with fast growths lining the asteroid avenues
        spreading out against velvety blackness,
          riding the non-vegetal sky.
            But the choir of chlorophyl voices,
nuclei of chromosomic harmonies, each green
trigger of light bouncing energy waves off another
    along the sinewy avenues,
        vines of stars! Howl of
          open spaces. The lush
    crawling hush of it.
      Audible silences.

These calyx-centers of slow-motion openings, petals
    in different speed-lengths, lipping their
      slow undercoil extremity-tips as they
point the way to an inward explosion
    of all greenery, silver-dazzle
      dew-sparkling it all in fizz of
        spray showers constantly

keeping it all moist, a noble
      sheen on the green, the purple and yellow
        alive, each color, each edge
lying next to each other in a
    space that is no-space, but whose

cool breath can be known. Breathing
is the name of the dance. The slow
    revolutions. There is a

deep-rooted spin at work here, a spin and a
casting off in chilled degrees of stillness
not seed, not generation as we know it, but a kind of
     non-generative multiplication, it actually
        just multiplies in sudden
            anticipation of simply
occupying not space exactly, but
pure number. And there is a symmetry.

This is the Garden.

Come recline in its shade.

Pinwheels of brightness descend.

You are alone here among the multitudes.

There is no one here but you.

2

The flower
of such a journey

it turns in a half light
like a celestial lettuce

leafy and full-bodied,
sits on the horizon

advertising itself.

It broadcasts its bloom.
There is nothing

quite like it. Vibrations
of miniscule motions

shudder petals so fragile
you would say they were

light itself.
So their flutter

is light within light.
No lettuce this,

but a rarer growth,
not an emblem,

not a symbolic rose,
but an expression of Garden

in one flower.
Something utterly beyond

imagination, but gathering up
in the splendor of its

beauty all the possible
longings of the heart for something

beyond the usual dimension
of magnificence, to a

one dot, a one full
flowering that is

almost visible but certainly
cognizable there

where it stays.

3

For the Arabs, a hot desert folk,
part of the allure of the Garden
is the reclining in shade,
drinking cool water poured by youths out of ewers,
and the meandering rivers of milk, of honey,
of a wine that doesn't intoxicate, a pure substance,
but the vision of deep shadow, and the word itself
for Garden in Arabic suggests
      pools of shade under thick bushes, branches
            offering cool grottos of shadow
in which one can get in out of any heat

of personal burning, certainly out from the
        heat of Hell.

For us, urban and northerly, perhaps this
opposite to what is here on earth is not quite so
vivid, but although we're not so
thirsty after grimy rides on caravans plodding almost
        indefinitely against featureless landscapes,
even though this may not be our immediate reality
how can Garden within Garden of coolness and refreshment
not appeal to our heart's thirst for a
place beyond the total hurly-burly of simply carrying on
past all landscapes of drama or terror which
               when compared with the
      next world are certainly featureless, like
        comparing an ant against the whole sky,

then the cool green shade-pools delight us
and there we can
      take our refuge and lie
        down.

Texas Power Apocalypse

ALLEN GINSBERG

We're driving south on the big Boulevard toward the Texas town, rising gigantic miles away down the arcaded roadway thru the Super Suburb Apartment Mall. On each side, factories and shopping marts are built up solid, so you can see the sky above but colonnades of industrial development alleys block off the rest of the landscape in mid-afternoon.

There are workmen and elevators and wires tiny in the distance up the sides of the electric power tower—10 times bigger than Empire State or Eiffel Tower buildings—where cables hang from the top for fixing the elevator & Dynamo stations at mid-level and trestle-leg side left, all which we can see clearly as we approach. All are controlled from the station & some solar power directs the flow of energy from sea-sunk wells to Florida generators to Oklahoma Power Stations—all the way from the Gulf of Mexico to the Mississippi.

We're driving due south to the Big City, Peter & I and Blake & a few others in our new black shiny truck. I notice a small sparkler-like series of blow-outs way up on the left side of the iron-strutted tower, maybe an elevator cable tangled is causing static electricity sparks to shower down the sides of the plat-form, or an acetylene torch has started a short circuit with blue & red flashing explosions up the side of a thick rubber wire-cable hanging alongside the eleva-tor platform. It's ominous I realize, the whole big structure's interconnected like a nervous system and one blow-out could set off a series of current-explosions rushing back & forth from station to station up and down the nodes & connec-tions of the entire perpendicular power-grid.

The sparks get more intense, glowing, there's a wire-meltdown, electric power's flowing out the side of the four-footed giant tower & showering down on the roofed streets below in shining liquid spark waterfalls, we stop the car to see the show—but it isn't a show, is it safe to be that close? We're ten miles away still, & the tower lifts up off earth way over our heads already—are we far enough away in case the electric shower rises up to the top of the tower & the head blows off & some wires melt & fall down like burning ropes?

We stop the car & pull over to the side under an arcade so that if any sparks or pieces of explosion fly outward over the suburbs we'll be safe right over our heads—but could fragments fall down on the roadway nearby? We get the car stopped by the building window-side protected by the roof that juts way out over our viaduct—we're at ground level & can still see the tiny conflagration amid electric wires on the east side of the power structure. We get out to look, it must be big news—

Suddenly there's a glaring explosion & distant boom of electric & the short circuit jumps across the platform on mid-lower level and a lightning-like silent snake of electric glows flashing across, connecting both sides of the tower—the legs & struts opposite blow up, there's a strange flow, a black black smoke streaming out, as if a strong fast wind poured thru the opposite side of the mid-level platform—an explosion Oh Oh. The fiery wire-flow of electric short-circuits straight up the tower & burns almost instantly to the head platform way up on top over our heads, way high up over the city, the entire tower-side cables and internal network of cables cybernetic up & down the stress points of the Texas High Tension Tower light up & begin sparking showering molten iron down like 4th of July meteors with red & blue sparkler tails—

Are we safe still? Falling iron begins flying slowly down thru the air—yes we're miles away, it's beautiful but dangerous? What about the people living nearby or closer, mile, a half mile away, O my God, what can they do, it must be awful, this is big enough so whole city blocks nearby can be crushed if it gets worse, & house roofs collapse just from little pieces of falling gigantic wires—

The right hand side of the tower blows outward with a blue lightning-like spark, it's terrible, awesome the fragmentation of the supports & guy wires & struts & elevator & power cables—the entire structure's no longer up on legs, it's toppling the higher needlepoint elevator & transmitter-head and mid-section is collapsing toward the right as we stand there and watch. Are we still far enough away? We never thought to see this—the builders never dreamed it could happen—the whole interconnected wire-net surging with red fire & electric liquid burning out the cables & connections, it's like the Hindenburg Zeppelin explosion way high up in the air, people jumping like flies from the gridwork & ribs of the structure—well this will be remembered in history! There we are safe on the ground, we're far enough away, the right hand side of the tower's completely collapsed & the whole top level miles long has slowly drifted buckled & fallen over opposite us to the right over the suburbs—where did we think we were headed? Will we be able to go back or around the city wreckage?

Boulder, August 18, 1979
6am

Roland Topor

Allen Ginsberg

COSMOPOLITAN GREETINGS

To Struga Festival Golden Wreath Laureates & International Bards 1986

Stand up against governments, against God.

Stay irresponsible.

Say only what we know & imagine.

Absolutes are Coercion.

Change is absolute.

Ordinary mind includes eternal perceptions.

Observe what's vivid.

Notice what you notice.

Catch yourself thinking.

Vividness is self-selecting.

If we don't show anyone, we're free to write anything.

Remember the future.

Freedom costs little in the U.S.

Advise only myself.

Don't drink yourself to death.

Two molecules clanking against each other require an observer to become scientific data.

The measuring instrument determines the appearance of the phenomenal world (after Einstein).

The universe is subjective.

Walt Whitman celebrated Person.

We are observer, measuring instrument, eye, subject, Person.

Universe is Person.

Inside skull is vast as outside skull.

What's in between thoughts?

Mind is outer space.

How do we talk to ourselves in bed at night, making no sound?

First thought, best thought.

Mind is shapely, Art is shapely.

Maximum information, minimum number of syllables.

Syntax condensed, sound is solid.

Intense fragments of spoken idiom, best.

Move with rhythm, roll with vowels.

Consonants around vowels make sense.

Savor vowels, appreciate consonants.

Subject is known by what she sees.

Others can measure their vision by what we see.

Candor ends paranoia.

from

Women Artists International

BETTY LADUKE

Milena Lah, in 1968–1973, created the first of three cycles of a 3½′ tall x 60′ long sculptural group, "The Form of Experience After the Fall of Icarus," thirty-four separate pieces of carved gypsum. She compares "The Fall of Icarus" with the history of Yugoslavia, its poems and myths, and the people's desire for freedom. She was influenced by early Greek sculpture, and she speaks of the Adriatic odyssey that moves from a biological to a spiritual, cosmic essence. Her spiraling forms are "magic-circles, the feelers of the universe."

Jagadamba Devi is from Jitwapur, Northern India, a small village with a community of women who maintain ancient folk traditions through painting. With a bold, personal style, Devi vitalizes popular themes and sacred images based on the ancient Hindu texts of Ramayana and Mahabharata, as we see in "Shiva" (1980) and "Krishna and the Cow." Devi learned traditional techniques for making paint and brushes to apply to mud walls, but now uses paper and synthetic materials to make her work more marketable. She was the 1978 recipient of the National Award for Artists of the Highest Order.

The vibrantly-colored batiks of **Nike Twins Seven Seven** express her interest in preserving Yoruba culture, history, and mythology. She has attained professional status as an artist, an unusual feat for a woman trained in traditional crafts. "Palm Wine Drinker" (1985) is a story-telling image of an eager trapper who scales a tree for palm wine, the national beverage, and is characteristic of her expressive treatment of the human form.

Born in 1905, **Lois Mailou Jones**, an associate of the Harlem Renaissance writers, won acclaim as an artist in spite of an environment of intense racial discrimination. She pioneered the use of an Afro-American idiom, and her recent African-inspired paintings incorporate images of masks and the human form. Earlier, in Haiti, she painted "Grand Bois d'Illet" (1953), a watercolor rich in the symbolism of voodoo.

Suzanne Wenger moved to Nigeria from Austria and adopted the religious beliefs of the Yoruba people in Oshogbo; in time, she was accepted as a cult priestess. She and five Yoruba artisans collaborated on sculptures for shrines in the sacred Osun grove, a tropical forest. These anthropormorphic gateways and walls, temple pieces, small wood carvings, and stone images along winding pathways and clearings express the Yoruba world view. One of the most impressive of them is the dynamic, free-standing "Iyamoopo Shrine," that soars over twenty feet high.

June Beer is from the remote jungle town, Bluefields, on Nicaragua's Atlantic coast. Her paintings document the life of Nicaragua's blacks who were brought as slaves from Africa and who remain on the Atlantic coast, a black, English-speaking region. On art and life, June Beer says: "I rave over everything, the moon, my flowers. It doesn't take too much to make me happy. Sometimes I see a little black child pass, and just wish I could keep her there until I paint her." "Dancers" (1983) exemplifies this joyous sensibility.

Jessica Hagedorn

THE SONG OF BULLETS

Formalized
by middle age
we avoid crowds
but still
love music.

Day after day
with less surprise
we sit
in apartments
and count
the dead.

Awake,
my daughter croons
her sudden cries
and growls
my new language.
While she sleeps
we memorize
a list of casualties:

The photographer's brother
the doctor is missing.
Or I could say:
"Victor's brother Oscar
has been gone for two years …
It's easier for the family
to think of him dead."

Victor sends
a Christmas card
from El Salvador:
"Things still the same."

And there are others
who don't play
by the rules—
someone else's brother
perhaps mine
languishes in a hospital;
everyone's grown tired
of his nightmares
and pretends
he's not there.

Someone else's father
perhaps mine
will be executed
when the time comes.
Someone else's mother
perhaps mine

telephones incessantly
her husband is absent
her son has gone mad
her lover has committed suicide
she's a survivor
who can't appreciate
herself.

The sight
of my daughter's
pink and luscious flesh
undoes me.
I fight
my weakening rage
I must remember
to commit
those names to memory
and stay angry.

Friends send postcards:
"Alternating between hectic
social Manila life & rural wonders
of Sagata ... on to Hongkong and Bangkok—
Love ... "

Assassins cruise the streets
in obstrusive limousines
sunbathers idle
on the beach

War is predicted
in five years
ten years
any day now
I always thought
it was already happening

snipers and poets locked
in a secret embrace
the country
my child may never see

a heritage
of women in heat
and men
skilled at betrayal

dancing
to the song
of bullets.

The Southern Front

ALEJANDRO MURGUIA

The *responsable* addressed them, his hands behind his back, his voice rolling out in the cool night air and entering every pore of Ulises.

"Compañeros. From now on you'll be called compañeros. You are here in a security house. As you well know the war is raging. Within the next day or two we will be sending all of you to a training camp. In the meantime you will stay here and train and perform other duties. There are some things here you must get used to right now; you will exercise rigorously to get in top condition, also, get rid of your underwear, a guerrilla goes without shorts, 'cause the heat and the conditions will only give you jock rash and you'll be worthless for long marches. There's one more thing, you are not to remove your boots under any circumstances, not even to sleep, understood? The guerrilla must be ready to move at any moment.

"Compañeros, I hope each of you have thought this out carefully, because from here on in there is no turning back. Once you enter a security house, the only way out is victory or death. You have now passed into a historical position, you are now part of the Southern Front, Benjamín Zeledon. As of this moment, you are under command of the general staff of this house and of this sector. Are there any questions compañeros? No questions? Then you may turn in for the night, that is all *compas*."

So you wanted to be a freedom fighter, Ulises said to himself, while the words of the *responsable* swirled in his head. Well, now you're in 'til it's over. For some reason the thought made him panic with doubt that he'd survive. But in his heart he knew it was the right thing being here. Chicano, Méjicano, Nicoya, the same ancient Nahua culture and language, the same struggle from Cuauhtemoc to Carlos Fonseca, even if others didn't understand it now, they'd understand it later. And if he did survive this little war, then what? He'd still like a crack at film, script, a modern version of the myth of Quetzalcoatl and his arch nemesis Tezcatlipoca. Set the two gods in an urban barrio, make the deities (without offense) Pachucos, have them speak in street talk *caló*, throw in some tropical music, say, Willie Colon and Ruben Blades. Sure he could make it work. When this was all over, maybe he'd get a chance at that project.

There's been lots of time once, when he could have done everything he ever wanted and more. But so much time had been wasted carousing, so that he could say he'd lived, if nothing else. Yeah, he'd lived all right, seriously, fast. The phrase reminded him of the time he drove Highway 99 from Lassen to L.A.; a sudden downpour stopped him in Sacramento and, drying out in the Reno bar, he met the young *chola* Beatrice, known as Pinky, who took him to the river where she undressed in the rain, and he had her on the wet, sandy banks of the Sacramento River. He stayed in Sacra a few days; later, they drove together to Los Angeles, making it every time they stopped for gas; in the front seat, the back seat, in the fields ripe with strawberries and grapes. Near Delano, they passed a procession of farmworkers led by the image of the Virgen de Guadalupe and a black eagle on a red banner, and he stopped the car and marched with them for miles. Pinky loved him all the more for it. He was 19 then, the "saint of the San Joaquin" with a black '58 Chevy.

Later there'd been San Francisco, with an endless succession of nights at The Club on Mission Street, dancing rumbas, drinking iced rums, pretty ladies sharing his table. After hours, the all night parties at the Macondo Club, then with the sun peeking over Potrero Hill, he'd go for breakfast at the Silver Crest where the wide-hipped waitress in soiled white uniform served him steak and eggs with strong black coffee. Early in the morning, when most people were at work, he would stretch his weary bones a few hours on the sofa and be ready to do it all over again that night.

That had been, for sure, the wildest time of his life. He was teaching at the state college and on weekends he'd drive north to the wine country in his red Triumph TR3. But best of all, he'd met Miriam, the woman he'd been in love with, in what now seemed like a dream of centuries ago. Miriam, he whispered her name to the night. He reached into his shirt pocket and withdrew the Polaroid photo of a smiling Latin woman, with hazel eyes and brown hair. Through Miriam was how he met the exiled Nicaraguans; Kiki the poet, Willie the pilot, Chombo, and many others, and from them he first heard of the Front and the struggle against the 45-year reign of the Somozas. One day Kiki gave him a letter from Carlos Fonseca, the leader of the Front (typed, probably, by Fonseca himself, from somewhere in Nicaragua, with his signature and seal), addressed to the Chicanos in the States, asking for support in the prolonged struggle. Kiki had told him then that one day Ulises would be in the mountains; and now here he was, his Georgia boots on and ready. Long before most people in the States had heard of this little country, he was in love with a woman whose mouth tasted of this land and whose spirit was like the cloud-veiled volcanos rising over the lakes.

Ulises thought of the city by the blue bay, saw himself sitting alone at the bar at Abu-Zam Zam's three days ago, drinking amber cognac in that Casablanca setting while old Bruno poured and discoursed on the decadence and failure that was Ulises' generation. Ulises' friends never roamed the Haight with flowers in their hair; most of his homeboys died young in barrio gang wars or in Southeast Asia, or rotted in prisons from Chino to San Quentin. He was the lone survivor of his barrio who had escaped that fate. Many in his generation now lived disengaged lives behind a facade of respectability, bought by jumping through the hoop, and still they failed with their good dreams and good intentions. In the streets of the barrios *vatos* were still killing each other; even more children ran ragged chasing hopeless dreams. And right this minute, in the hallowed corridors of the CIA or in the murky depths of Foggy Bottom, some career desk man was no doubt planning the next Project Phoenix or invasion of the Caribbean or Central America with all the lost, wasted blood of Nam forgotten. The ones who went to Nam and survived the horror of it were never the same. In other times, the youth of a generation had fought against Fascism in Spain; the young men of his era were asked to kill peasants and rice farmers who didn't even know why they were being slaughtered. Was his generation a waste from a moral point of view? Maybe that's why Ulises, along with a half-dozen other Chicanos from the Valle and from Los had come to the front to salvage the honor of a whole generation. There was no carpet bombing by B-52s here, just people like himself, with light arms and automatic weapons trying to kill you and you trying to kill them. He'd always believed that once in a person's life (without being drafted or impressed), you had to be willing to risk everything for what you believed was right and good, even beautiful.

He'd known many places: sprawling East L.A. dotted with hills and palm trees, the clubs on Cahuenga where he'd spent many a night at the Manne Hole listening to the greats like Cannonball Adderly wailing saxophone jazz, or feeling the cool blue breezes of the Pacific at the Lighthouse; New York, fast and furious, where five bucks got you into the Corso to dance all night with the beautiful Puerto Rican women swirling in circles on the dance floor to the bands of Pacheco and Fajardo. Mexico City was greatest once, now suffocated in *mal aires*, though he'd always have the Opera Cafe with its white-coated waiters and its 1920s decor. At the National Palace in the Zocalo, he saw himself in Rivera's murals, the battle scene where Jaguar warriors fought the invading Spaniards. But in the end he'd gone back to his barrio by the bay and the one woman that should have always been his—Miriam.

He wondered how he would react under fire. His grandfather had fought in the Mexican Revolution. An aunt on his father's side, one time homecoming queen of Jalisco, had died of malaria nursing the wounded of Madrid during the Spanish civil war. His uncle Agustin on his mother's side, survived a sniper's bullet on Iwo Jima, and his older brother earned a Silver Star during the Tet Offensive and later a Purple Heart. Armando tasted the Nica insurrection of September and Danilo had seen Nam; but Ulises had been left behind when they went to the front. Now he was following the same road. He could run five miles uphill, do forty push-ups on his knuckles, spar three rounds, assemble an

M-1 blindfolded, and hit the bull's-eye at a 100 meters. He was as ready as he was ever going to be. As ready as Toño would have wanted him to be. Toño, the 19-year-old Nica who passed briefly through the States, inspiring many of them with his discipline and morale. Toño, ex-student of Garfield High in East L.A., homeboy, the military hero in the takeover of Rivas the year before, who'd led the assault squad at Peñas Blancas armed with a bazooka. Toño now dead.

The starlight disappeared as the truck passed under a thick net of branches. The trucks came to a halt. Inside the canvas top, the air turned hot and muggy. Chains cranking brought the back gate down, the tarp was lifted, letting in breezy air. One by one, the *compas* jumped out the back, landing with a squat on the asphalt road. The moon had been covered by clouds, a low mist hugged the ground. Only shadows moved among shadows.

As Ulises' eyes got used to the dark, he could make out the square block forms of buildings along the highway. Out of the black ink of the shadows, *compas* appeared with rifles strapped across their chests, floppy jungle hats pulled low. The two columns were formed, Ulises' platoon at the head of them, and led to a nearby abandoned building with long sloping roof and many windows. Giant guanacaste trees surrounded the buildings and ominous silence filled the stagnant air.

The 150 men and women in the columns were led single file beside the stucco walls and concrete landing of the abandoned Costa Rica customs building. The border with Nicaragua was 500 meters away. Ulises was at the head of the columns, nearest the border. He placed the FAL between himself and Gaspar and used his knapsack and beret as a pillow to rest his head. His back against the concrete, Ulises ran his hand down the smooth stock of the FAL named Miriam. No one knew what the morning would bring; Ulises closed his eyes and fell into a deep sleep.

His sleep was filled with disturbing dreams of the past. Miriam appeared just beyond his outstretched arms, talking to him in that strange dream way, but he couldn't quite hear, so she came closer and closer, Ulises reaching for her with open arms.

The bright white flash of a mortar explosion twenty meters away and the dull metallic BAHGON! sound of the shock-wave hit him simultaneously, slamming his eyes open and shaking the branches of the trees above. The blast shook up everyone. Gaspar reached out a hand to touch him. "You all right Ulises?"

"Yes, I'm all right." He didn't say his heart was beating a 100 miles an hour. He was stunned by how loud the explosion had been, and found himself short of breath, his heart beating rapidly. It took him a moment to recover and become fully awake from the dream. Then he felt something odd. Putting his right hand down his pants, he felt the stickiness in his groin. Jesus, he thought, I just had a wet dream. My god, how long's it been? He withdrew his moist fingers. It was the dream of Miriam, at the same time as the explosion. A sudden rush of sadness and nostalgia overpowered him in the hollow ringing left after the explosion. Every emotion he'd ever felt about Miriam came at him, confusing and disturbing, and with the driftwood from the past came a crazy, irrational fear that made him feel like running away, hiding in the dark hills.

With the quieting of the leaves, the smell of burnt gunpowder drifted to them. Ulises could feel the tauntness of the column. His own senses became fine-tuned, making him hypersensitive to his surroundings. He could have picked out the footsteps of an ant on a leaf above. Gaspar, stretched out rigid as a board, glanced over to Ulises. "Do you think they'll keep hitting us?"

Ulises remembered something that Che said in the diary.

"There's nothing you can do about it," he answered. "The chances of a direct hit by a mortar are very slim. So why worry? Best thing would be to get some sleep."

"You can sleep through this?"

"Have to. Don't want to waste energy, might need it in the morning."

Gaspar sighed and lay back down. The landscape was still; with it came the tenseness of waiting for the next shell to fall. Ulises turned on his side, his face in the knapsack, his hands covering his face, the black FAL resting at his side, like the woman who used to sleep next to him.

The booming of mortars started again. The white phosphorus flash of the explosions were landing far away, followed a few seconds later by the hollow metal thud of the sound wave. The fire line was moving away from them. Ulises propped himself up on one elbow and watched the fireballs landing on a distant hill. The first explosion had shocked him, sent his heart racing, now the beat was steady and calm, he'd gotten over the shock. But that first instant of the explosion, his life had flashed before him and he felt lucky to have seen it all go by so fast. It was only supposed to happen when you were dying. He knew he couldn't sleep now. It was nearing 0500 hours. The approaching whine of a solitary shell came tearing through the treetops and he covered himself with his arms as it landed not far from where the first shell had exploded. The shrapnel tore the leaves above him into shreds. Gaspar sat upright as if wanting to bolt.

"Calm down," Ulises said. "Don't make yourself a target."

Gaspar laid down again. Ulises, the echo of the barrage sounding in his ears, knew now he would not run, he would hold his ground when the time came, he waited at the head of the column, with the cold calm of the warrior, for daybreak on the border.

ERNESTO CARDENAL

Translated from the Spanish by Jonathan Cohen

AMONG FACADES

We're going through the streets of a neighborhood in New York,
small shops, a restaurant, *Dry Cleaning*,
apartment houses, three-, four-stories high,
made of red brick, concrete, gray brick,
                              then we're passing through a hamlet in the Alps,
                    cobblestone streets in a Mexican village,
then a river with a medieval mill,
                        a dusty street in a town in the West,
               with its saloons, a window with broken glass,
on a hill an 11th-century castle,
and once again apartment houses, a bank, liquor stores
                    in any city in the United States,
but if you knock on anything, it sounds hollow,
                         everything is plasterwork,
              they're only the outside walls, there's nothing in back.
A policeman in the middle of the street, with his badge
                        and book for giving out tickets,
might be a real policeman or a famous actor.
And the producer who is showing me everything tells me:
"no director, no producer, nobody
                                      runs the show in a movie
                    —the bank that's financing it does."
And on leaving and seeing the banks, restaurants, *Dry Cleaning*,
I thought whatever I'd knock on would sound hollow,
Hollywood, all of Los Angeles, everything
                    was merely walls
                                      with nothing in back.

MALTA

This is Malta.
Big ships in the harbor
      with black hulls and white on top,
as big as the fortifications near them,
and the fortress also thrusting its walls into the sea like ships' bows.
Yellow walls of the Knights of Malta.
        Ramparts
          built on ramparts.
   The Mediterranean:
blue turning white on the rocks.
      And huge round towers on top of these walls.
The sea was closed off here with a chain
when there were corsairs.
Old narrow streets over there
with lots of tv antennas.
    Out to the horizon
"sea the color of wine" according to Homer
—but does a blue wine exist?
     In twelve different shades of blue.
Or where the blue turns into green and the green into foam.
Or:
Swells building up
   green with white
       striped-looking waves.
Beaches so clear you don't see water, just seaweed
on the bottom.
      Opposite Calypso's island
where Ulysses was held captive six years.
     There weren't any tour guides then.
In a dark blue harbor
     fishing boats
with the eyes of Osiris painted on their bows
      near the yachts.
It's not the tourist season now.
The water is cold.

In a grotto the water
            fluorescent blue
       where before sirens used to be seen.
And you still can easily think you're seeing them
when the sand on the bottom refracts the sunlight, making it rose- and
    mallow-colored.
But they only used to sing in the nighttime.
And you still can easily think you're hearing them
when the night wind is whistling through a cave.
      Houses a pale, light color.
           With flat rooftops against an arid background.
Saint Paul was shipwrecked here in 60 A.D.
maybe in front of that hotel.
The clover makes the March fields look pink.
      Sea glimpsed in among a pine grove.
        Island of honey and roses, Cicero called it.
With hardly any soil, the ground mostly stones,
          the whole countryside crisscrossed by stone fences
and loaded with cactus Columbus brought.
Very close, behind Calypso's little island,
Pershing Missiles, on Sicily, menacing.
A little village below the cliffs
where there are simple restaurants.
          And right by the huge stone temple
              hot dogs.
Tiny island shaped like a fish
that all the empires wanted for themselves,
Romans, Ottomans, Napoleon, Nelson, OTAN:
free and at peace for the first time since the Phoenicians
now with an international meeting of pacifists and guerrillas
where I planted, for Nicaragua, an olive tree.

Julian Beck (1925-1985)

ERIC BENTLEY

Julian Beck died of cancer on September 14th. The illness had been long-drawn-out and painful. His life had not been an easy one, even before. On the contrary. And yet I see it, intending no irony, as a success story. With the sixty years granted to him, Julian did what he wanted to do.

To be sure, that is not the same as achieving what he wanted to achieve. He wanted to transform the world. In this autumn of 1985, it stands untransformed, or, worse, transformed in just the opposite way from what Julian wished. The point is that he was not deterred by the strong possibility of total failure. To be so deterred (as he saw things) would simply be to fail. He had faith in the possibility of total success. He was Utopian. Quite consciously and gladly: which meant that there was a paradise accessible, not just externally and at the end of time but, in his heart, and today—"paradise now."

He did what he wanted to do: with his wife Judith Malina he created the Living Theatre which, if it was not a new macrocosm, was a new microcosm. Not an ivory tower, however: a headquarters of revolution, a guerrilla theater, though a pacifist one. This is not the place to write the history of the Living Theatre. It has already been written; and will be written again. All I can hope to do is report an experience of that theater and of Julian.

We knew each other—not well, but we were well aware of each other—for about thirty-six years. There was a moment, at lunch in the Hans Jaeger restaurant in Yorkville in 1951, when Julian and I almost joined forces. As Judith reported in her *Diary*: "Eric Bentley ... wishes to direct a play for the Living Theatre if he likes the early work." Instead, our lives took different paths, intersecting, sometimes in strife, over the course of the decades.

Nineteen sixty two marked the Battle of Brecht. *A Man's a Man* was a topical play at the time of the Cuban missile crisis, and I planned to put it on. So did the Living Theatre. And there were two productions, opening in New York on successive nights. A good idea, really: it should be tried with other plays. But the two production outfits did battle with each other. The curious can consult the files of *The Village Voice* (which took the side of the Living Theatre against me and mine).

The next clash came in '68 when *The New York Times* stuck this title on a piece of mine: "I Reject the Living Theatre." The piece said that the LT was making us all a "take-it-or-leave-it" offer, and I was gonna leave it. The topic, of course, was tactics. I thought that the LT's tactics were going to "turn off" the very people they wanted to "turn on." And this was a practical and political matter. The aim was to stop the Vietnam War. Enacting "paradise now"—orgasms for all who could manage them on the stage of the Brooklyn Academy—did not seem to me to be the way. Especially as, along with the "love" being so lavishly offered, there came—it wasn't quite clear how or why—much ill-will and even hate. In this period I refused to speak at a meeting of "Theatre of Ideas" because I got word that the LT was going to break it up. (The LT did so.) And yet it was in this same period of maximum discord that I formed a positive relationship with the Becks.

Meanwhile, my *Times* piece had brought me fan mail I could have done without: "with friends like that, who needs ... ?" One letter made me think. It was from a respected colleague who said I was right—but then the LT did have certain technical and aesthetic virtues I hadn't mentioned. *Touché*. But how about the implication that the LT was to be vindicated by the ordinary aesthetic standards—there was "good theater" here and there, they did know their job, even had a little originality etcetera? To think in this way would be to reject, not just their tactics, but their whole *raison d'être*: the connection, declared in the word "living," which they wished to make between theater and life.

I was beginning to regret, not what I had said in *The Times*, but that I had said it in *The Times*, which is no place for what should be the intramural debates of radicals. The answer, I thought, was to get together with the Becks and have it all out face to face. I believe they arrived at the same idea independently. We certainly got together, and something even better than "having it all out" took place: a meeting of hearts and minds. I'd say it was at this meeting that we really became friends for life, an item essential to the story I'm telling. Some of the love the LT had been offering in the theater had seemed abstract or ambivalent—and definitely had a capital L. To know Julian and Judith was to learn that concrete love—with a small l—was at the center of their lives and work. This is what eternally separates them from show business or any other business.

Julian, by the way, had first-rate qualifications as a professional. He was one of the best stage designers of his time, and could have made a name as a painter, if that had been what he wanted. He was a good writer, both as poet (*Twenty-One Songs of the Revolution*) and as drama theorist and chronicler (*The Life of the Theatre*). He was a fine director, and as an actor was still growing in his fifties. In Paolo Pasolini's film *Oedipus*, though Julian's voice was unhappily not used, his performance still stood out magnificently from the rest. I have not seen the film he made in Italy about a rabbi who is being tortured by the Spanish Inquisition (*Destruction of Hope*, based on a story by Villiers de l'Isle Adam), but the stills I have seen reveal a noble intensity.

You could guess from such quotes that Julian was an actor, and a pro at that. But you could also guess he was more. By the time people are forty, as Camus said, they have the face they deserve. When one says Julian was beautiful, one is not congratulating him on good looks. One is not talking aesthetics, one is talking existence. And even the confrontation of non-existence: Julian was never more beautiful than at sixty, looking death in the eye. Suffering was there. The well-shaped cheekbones and skull seemed almost to come through the skin, but there was also the nobility of victory over suffering and the old glint in his eye that betokened his interest in *you*—the person he was looking at, feeling interested in, concerned for. He was not a saint, and wouldn't want to be called one. But there was a spiritual purity about him all the same. To be with him was to breathe mountain air. I have derived that particular lift, that exhilaration, from only one other person, someone Julian respected: the writer Barbara Deming. He resembled Barbara, spiritually speaking, more than he resembled anyone in the theater. He didn't get the kind of death anyone could want but he had had the life he wanted. The world had not been changed, yet he had done all a man can do to change it. So, to that extent, it had, too, been changed. How Julian changed himself! Look back from the photos of the dying hero of 1984-85 (again: no irony) to photos of Julian, the rich boy of the forties. Now *there's* a transformation! And how could he transform himself in such a way without transforming others? Others were indeed transformed, and even those he casually touched—either directly or from stage or screen—were permanently affected. For, as he himself put it: "I cut the curtains of deception, beautiful, so that we can go through together where no one can go through alone."

When such a life has been lived, who dares say theater is just a business? Who dares say it is just an art?

Meditation on Theatre

JULIAN BECK

thirty years creating political theatre.

thirty years in a movement going on already how long, over a hundred and thirty years, many names, the story of the social uses of the drama. (read emma goldman: she talks about hauptmann, brieux, tolstoi, gorki, we know all about that, and we know also about meyerhold, futurism, constructivism, the federal theatre, mayakovsky, the blaue bluse. all those things.

the political theatre of judith malina and i, 1947, was projected against a political reality which, as we all know, defies, in fact, the epic powers of literature to make clear to the human mind the cataclysmic implications of its dimension. quantities of death. the 80,000,000 total toll of world war II, the 6 million jews, the 300,000 japanese of hiroshima nagasaki. climates of racism, rampant colonialism, the whole world of work and labor locked in obedience to a culture which cultivates limitation. with this as the scenery we projected a theatre.

the popular cultural ambience in that period maintained that politics cancelled the art of the theatre. piscator heard this often. paid no attention.

erwin piscator, judith's teacher 1945-1947, speaking always of political theatre, projecting maps and newsreels during his productions that we might be aware of how it is all linked together. he was often accused of emphasizing what people already knew, but it was untrue. people did not know the link, and do not all know it still.

the theatre of 1979 projected against a background of radioactive sky. the political scenery now, the climate of disaster, the ceaseless procession of violence thru the '50s, the '60s, the '70s, genocides and little murders, impels the theatre no less than ever to pause and reconsider. what's going on?

1979. the emarginated gather their forces to oppose the construction of nuclear energy centers. here the ecological movement unites and enters into action.

197

meanwhile cracks in reactors are spotted everywhere, every day newspapers report discoveries of further accidents past and present. concealment. and in the margins of italy germany spain france holland i can report that there are hundreds and hundreds of sprouting anarchist groups. can this be considered a tendency, a pendular swing towards a desire for liberty? i suspect in fact that it is. but we cannot live forever swinging back and forth between the extremes of a little liberty or its awful lack.

speculate. speculate further. stand at the rail of ship and peer out.

thirty years creating political theatre. the theatre is in the world, the world is in the theatre, the theatre is in the streets, streets in theatre. and all along the objective is unification. therefore all the efforts to find ways to rouse the public, making way for entrance, participation, the famous co-involvement, sense of life, of being at one, of acting together. and today, yes, there is increased conscious awareness, more groups and individuals taking lively part in the serious process of the creation of the world, that is, humankind is going through a transition from a passive state to an active state, from being acted upon to acting.

thirty years politicizing our own consciousness, sexual and racial awareness, third world tune-in, economic observation, starvation statistics, study of structures, group relationships, historical struggle, theory of flight.

first we thought: change the form, and the content will change. out came dada. in painting and sculpture and in theatre a hundred lofty attempts to describe and imply new relationships. the form changed. the content of life, how did it change?

it was necessary to change the form because no spectator can believe that the content can change if, at the same time, form remains the same. we are too logical. so a play that talks about change must reflect change in its form. if the form can change, so can content.

the theatre of our time is replete with stylistic invention. style must not be confused with form and the political sky behind the stage is still hung with menace. the threats of falling sky laboratories hang here tonight. and what will they hang there tomorrow?

we are in a period in which the individuation of style and the high degree of invention found in theatre proclaims again human diversity. how does this serve to clear the sky? it triggers release of fantasy and of identity. do we not go to the theatre in the midst of a life in which fantasy and identity are greatly repressed in order to relocate and release this fantasy? but now fantasy and identity are beginning to leak out. no one plan, no one work is responsible, this is a collective and international conspiracy on the part of artists hard at work for over a hundred years. the next dimension must be the combination of political conceptualization with liberated fantasy rather than with manifest male ego concerned with manipulation of power.

we arrived by coagulation of experience and awareness late in the '60s. over the gate, the inscription: strategy furthers, organization furthers, struggle furthers. and still chariots lurched thru the streets, armies marched into forests, cities were destroyed, deserts invaded, rivers in africa and asia turned red, bullets riddled the horizon, bombs exploded leaping from fingers of generals and terrorists who cried out, you give us no alternative.

and tho hundreds of theatres poured into the streets in the '70s, despair began to spread. people fainted, fell back, came to weeping in their lofts. nothing works, revolutions fail, nothing happens, the world is breaking down, it's cracking and we're going to get it.

work on what has been spoiled. if our strategies have failed and strategies mean the form, then we must change the form. meditate. invent. meditate. listen for the sound of human humming.

the mass media interrupt and broadcast predictions and analyses *reflusso*, a flowing back, returning to the past, the recent past, back to the stances of the '50s when a frightened world, holocausted, blinking from a-bomb flash, scared of repeated history and cold war postures and lies, tried to believe all the banalities of the culture, to pattern behavior on limited concepts, to believe what is easy to believe because what is hard to believe had burned out people's wits.

all these years of effort, and much will yet change, but not enough has yet changed, a hundred years of political theatre, thirty years of political theatre, marches, protests, movement activity, art, poems scattered every night, but the phenomena of militarism congest every detail, the backdrop is still full of all the scary images and there's all this dying, boats full of fleeing people sent back into the sea to drown, this starvation, this capital punishment. in our play "frankenstein" we conceived the definition of historical conditions as best symbolized by a series of executions: hanging, the garotte, the electric chair, the gas chamber, the guillotine, the firing squad, the torture rack, the block, and the victims all screaming i don't want to die, and every spectator cringed in shame, and it is still going on.

examine everything. leave nothing unturned. the structure more than ever pretending to be immutable, impervious, is more than ever atilt. what possibilities remain? if we even suspect that our techniques maintain the culture tho they speak out against it, then we must change the techniques. what does that mean change the techniques?

today i detect at last and declare it, a mounting distaste for rhetoric. almost ten years ago judith saying, it can't succeed with that rhetoric. now the distaste for rhetoric is becoming general. no one wants to hear it. we cannot use language and we cannot train our minds to think that way, else our actions will reflect it. they have and do.

we are in the crúcial zone again. from islands, voices. floating, emitting signals, like sirens, singing. calling over great distances. static. what? what? can't hear each other. judith: there's this immense thick glass wall between us and our visions. how do we get thru? militance and paramilitarism have not brought us through.

change the language. language as theatre's chief tool, language of mouth, of body. we developed the language of the body. artaud cried burn the texts to get us thru. words no longer told the truth. go at it again. change the language. no more dehumanization. thirty years creating political theatre. speak with human voice. don't move so fast. demilitarize even the theatre.

what does that mean, demilitarize the theatre? it might mean not to conceive it as a weapon, not to use it for attack. not to use it in any way it could extend the values, the psychology and sexology of a military culture. to think in non-military terms till we act in non-military ways.

what are we doing now? we are emitting signals. we are signalling that we are beginning again. Again along the lines of light.

London, 2 August 1979
From *Theandric*

LAWRENCE FERLINGHETTI

A Modest Proposal
To Change the Names of
Certain Streets in San Francisco

To be presented to
the Board of Supervisors of San Francisco

WHEREAS San Francisco's literary and artistic heritage should be made more visible and better known;

And WHEREAS many of its illustrious authors and artists, both remote and recent, have received no official recognition by the City;

And WHEREAS it would cost the City relatively very little to recognize them by renaming certain *very short* streets after them;

It is hereby proposed that the following streets or alleys be renamed after the following persons.

The presently **UNNAMED** alley between the red-brick building at 615 Third Street and the MJB Building at 665 Third Street (between Townsend and Brannan Streets) to be called **JACK LONDON ALLEY**. To quote Don Herron's *Literary World of San Francisco*: "On January 12, 1953, the 77th anniversary of his birth, the California Historical Society installed this plaque [at 601 Third Street] to mark the place Jack London was born in 1876. As the plaque states, "The original home on this site, then known as 615 Third Street, was destroyed in the fire of April 18, 1906." The London home was a two-story dwelling, one of a row of seven houses numbered 615-627; this row began, according to insurance maps of 1887, some 120 feet south of Brannan. Controversy still rages among London buffs, with many insisting the plaque should have been placed on the *current* 615 Third Street—a red-brick building erected in 1908—located next to the bank." The naming of the above alley will go far toward settling the dispute since it is located right next to the red brick building.

ADELAIDE ALLEY (a half block long) to be called **ISADORA DUNCAN STREET.** This is within a block of where she was born. On the west side of Taylor Street between Geary and Post, Adelaide is first listed in the 1861 San Francisco *Block Book,* but there is no information as to the name. There is some surmise that the street was named after a ship of that name, although it is not near the water.

ADLER ALLEY to be called **JACK KEROUAC ALLEY.** This little alley between Grant Avenue and Columbus Avenue runs between City Lights Bookstore and Vesuvio's bar, where Kerouac spent much time when in town. Adler Alley is listed on microfilm records for 1856. The 1856 San Francisco *City Directory* lists several Adlers but all are several blocks away. The street was probably named before 1856, but there is no record of who Adler was.

Extension of ADLER ALLEY to be called **HENRI LENOIR PLACE.** This little cul-de-sac is separated from the above part of Adler Alley by Columbus Avenue. It is directly in front of Spec's bar, the successor to the Twelve Adler bar founded by Lenoir at that location. He also founded Vesuvio's and still lives in this block. He is an art connoisseur and San Francisco's most famous bohemian.

ALDRICH STREET (two blocks long) to be called **AMBROSE BIERCE STREET.** Aldrich is directly behind the old San Francisco *Examiner* building at Third and Market, where Bierce was a columnist. The street was named after Mark Aldrich (1801-1873), according to Louis Loewenstein's *Streets of San Francisco:* "Although Aldrich's life was colorful, no one knows why he was so honored."

AUSTIN STREET (five blocks long) to be called **FRANK NORRIS STREET.** This is the neighborhood of Norris' novel *McTeague.* (The name-change can be limited to just the end of Austin Street, the Easternmost block between Polk and Larkin Streets.) Austin Street is first listed in the 1862 *City Directory.* An

Emillus Austin and a tinsmith, B.C. Austin, are listed. The latter lived near-by on Bush Street near Franklin. Otherwise there is no record of the name.

GROVER PLACE (a half block long) to be called **BENIAMINO BUFANO STREET.** Bufano, the famous Italian-American sculptor, worked and lived in various locations in North Beach. For some time he had a studio at Powell and Greenwich Streets adjoining Grover Place. In 1909, the street was named Gaven Place. In the 1910 *City Directory* it is changed to Grover. There are no Gavens or Grovers in the 1909 *Block Book,* but a Lee Grover, watchman, is listed at 2100 Greenwich Street that year.

The Westernmost (half) block of **COMMERCIAL STREET** to be called **MARK TWAIN PLACE.** This block terminates at the Transamerica Pyramid, the site of the former Montgomery Building (The Monkey Block) where Twain met a man named Tom Sawyer, whose name he adopted for his most famous novel. This block has already been closed off and turned into a plaza (unnamed).

HARWOOD ALLEY (a quarter block long) to be named **BOB KAUFMAN ALLEY.** The late legendary poet (known as "the American Rimbaud") lived close-by for many years. Off Filbert Street between Grant and Kearny, this alley was first listed in the 1864 *City Directory,* when the name was changed from Grand Place. In 1864, a John Harwood, carpenter, was living nearby at 416 Greenwich Street. In 1867-1870, a Thomas Harwood, carpenter and builder, was listed at the same address. According to a deed found at the California Historical Society, on August 6, 1851, Thomas Harwood bought the property adjoining Grand Place from a George Tame.

The Northernmost (half) block at the very end of **LEAVENWORTH STREET** to be called **RICHARD HENRY DANA PLACE.** This lies between Jefferson Street and the water at Fisherman's Wharf, and adjoins the Historic Ships anchorage, a fitting location for the author of *Two Years Before the Mast.*

MARY STREET (one block long) to be called **HERB CAEN LANE.** This alley is right next to the San Francisco *Chronicle.* This street, according to Loewen-stein's *Streets of San Francisco,* was "named for a friend or relative of a pioneer." (Or perhaps a dancehall queen.)

MONROE STREET (one block long) to be called **DASHIELL HAMMETT STREET**. Hammett lived at 20 Monroe Street in the 1920s. Perhaps named after James Monroe (1758-1831), fifth President of the United States. This is pure conjecture, there being no records to substantiate it.

NOBLES ALLEY (a quarter block long) to be called **RICHARD BRAUTIGAN ALLEY**. This is at the heart of Brautigan's old neighborhood, off Grant Avenue between Union and Filbert Streets. Named before 1856, perhaps after Father Giovanni Nobili (1812-1856), attached to the church of St. Francis of Assisi in the neighborhood. Myrick's *San Francisco's Telegraph Hill* says Nobili was changed to Nobles, but gives no date. (Brautigan, best known for his novel, *Trout Fishing in America*, died in 1984.)

ROMOLO STREET (a half block long) to be called **WILLIAM SAROYAN STREET**. This alley intersects Fresno Alley. Fresno was Saroyan's birthplace. Saroyan's most famous play, *The Time of Your Life,* took place at Izzy Gomez' saloon nearby in North Beach. There never was a Romolo connected with this street. It was listed as Pinkney Street until 1914. In the 1915 *City Directory* it is listed as "Pinkney—now Romo Place." A Fred Romo was listed in the 1917 *City Directory* as manager of a hotel in Romo Place, with his residence at 11 Romo Place. Romo was changed to Romolo in the 1922 *City Directory.*

TRACY PLACE (a quarter block long) to be called **KENNETH REXROTH PLACE**. This is in the heart of North Beach where Rexroth lived in the 1930s. He was certainly the most important critic, philosopher and poet to live in San Francisco in the 1950s & 60s, a kind of *pater familias* to younger generations. Tracy Place was known as Vallejo Alley until 1910. There is no trace of a Tracy in Italian North Beach in the City Directories of that time.

Research by Karen Larsen Associates

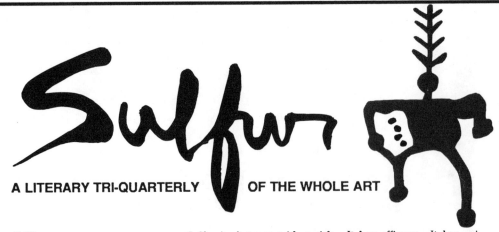

Sulfur

A LITERARY TRI-QUARTERLY **OF THE WHOLE ART**

Editor
CLAYTON ESHLEMAN

Contributing Editors
CLARK COOLIDGE
MICHAEL PALMER
ELIOT WEINBERGER
JOHN YAU

Correspondents
CHARLES BERNSTEIN
JAMES CLIFFORD
MARJORIE PERLOFF
JED RASULA
JEROME ROTHENBERG

Managing Editor
CARYL ESHLEMAN

Sulfur is Antaeus with a risk. It has efficacy. It has primacy. It is one of the few magazines that is more than a receptacle of talent, actually contributing to the shape of present day literary engagement.
— George Butterick

Sulfur must certainly be the most important literary magazine which has explored and extended the boundaries of poetry. Eshleman has a nose for smelling out what was going to happen next in the ceaseless evolution of the living art.
— James Laughlin

In an era of literary conservatism and sectarianism, the broad commitment of *Sulfur* to both literary excellence and a broad interdisciplinary, unbought humanistic engagement with the art of poetry has been invaluable. Its critical articles have been the sharpest going over the last several years.
— Gary Snyder

Founded at the California Institute of Technology in 1981, Sulfur magazine is now based at Eastern Michigan University. It appears 3 times a year, averages 200 pages per issue, and includes poetry by established post World War II poets (Olson, Duncan, Ginsberg) as well as younger writers, archival materials (Pound, Williams, Crane), translations (Artaud, Césaire, Paz), artwork (Golub, Petlin, Kitaj), and a 60 page section per issue of notes, correspondence and book reviews. A sample back issue is yours for the asking; back issues are available; a subscription is $15 a year for individuals, $22 for libraries and institutions.

Frank

An International Journal of

Contemporary Writing & Art

Issue 6/7   Edited in Paris in English

- **John Berger**   - **E.M. Cioran**
- **Hélène Cixous**   - **Robert Coover**
        - **Edmond Jabès**

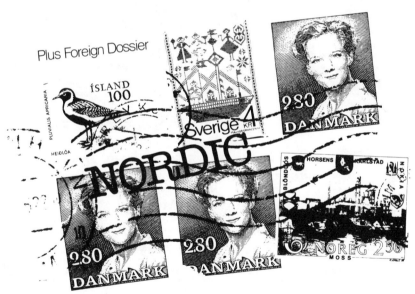

Plus Foreign Dossier

NORDIC

- -
Subscribe Today !
4 Issues (2 years): 125 FF / $15 US / £12 / $20 CD / $25 AUD / 45 DM

Name_____ Address_____
_____

David Applefield, Editor   6, rue Monge • 75005 Paris / France

CITY LIGHTS PUBLICATIONS

Angulo, J. de. *JAIME IN TAOS*
Antler. *FACTORY*
Artaud, Antonin. *ANTHOLOGY*
Bataille, Georges. *EROTISM: DEATH & SENSUALITY*
Baudelaire, Charles. *INTIMATE JOURNALS*
Bowles, Paul. *A HUNDRED CAMELS IN THE COURTYARD*
Brea, Juan & Mary Low. *RED SPANISH NOTEBOOK*
Brecht, Stefan. *POEMS*
Broughton, James. *SEEING THE LIGHT*
Buckley, Lord. *HIPARAMA OF THE CLASSICS*
Buhle, Paul (ed). *FREE SPIRITS: Annals of the Insurgent Imagination*
Bukowski, Charles. *THE MOST BEAUTIFUL WOMAN IN TOWN*
Bukowski, Charles. *NOTES OF A DIRTY OLD MAN*
Bukowski, Charles. *TALES OF ORDINARY MADNESS*
Burroughs, William S. *THE BURROUGHS FILE*
Burroughs, William S. *ROOSEVELT AFTER INAUGURATION*
Burroughs, William S. & Allen Ginsberg. *THE YAGE LETTERS*
Cardenal, Ernesto. *FROM NICARAGUA WITH LOVE*
Carrington, Leonora. *THE HEARING TRUMPET*
Cassady, Neal. *THE FIRST THIRD*
CITY LIGHTS JOURNAL No. 4
Ferlinghetti, Lawrence & Nancy J. Peters. *CITY LIGHTS REVIEW No. 1*
Choukri, M. *FOR BREAD ALONE*
Corso, Gregory. *GASOLINE/VESTAL LADY ON BRATTLE*
David-Neel, Alexandra. *SECRET ORAL TEACHINGS IN TIBETAN BUDDHIST SECTS*
Di Prima, Diane. *REVOLUTIONARY LETTERS*
Doolittle, Hilda (H.D.). *NOTES ON THOUGHT & VISION*
Duncan, Isadora. *ISADORA SPEAKS*
Duras, Marguerite. *MARGUERITE DURAS & OTHERS* (due 9/87)
Eberhardt, Isabelle. *THE OBLIVION SEEKERS*
Fenollosa, Ernest. *THE CHINESE WRITTEN CHARACTER AS A MEDIUM FOR POETRY*
Ferlinghetti, Lawrence. *LEAVES OF LIFE*
Ferlinghetti, Lawrence. *SEVEN DAYS IN NICARAGUA LIBRE*
Ferlinghetti, Lawrence. *PICTURES OF THE GONE WORLD*
Gascoyne, David. *A SHORT SURVEY OF SURREALISM*
Ginsberg, Allen. *THE FALL OF AMERICA*
Ginsberg, Allen. *HOWL AND OTHER POEMS*
Ginsberg, Allen. *INDIAN JOURNALS*
Ginsberg, Allen. *IRON HORSE*
Ginsberg, Allen. *KADDISH*
Ginsberg, Allen. *MIND BREATHS*
Ginsberg, Allen. *PLANET NEWS*
Ginsberg, Allen. *PLUTONIAN ODE.*
Ginsberg, Allen. *REALITY SANDWICHES*
Ginsberg, Allen. *SCENES ALONG THE ROAD*
Hayton-Keeva, S. *VALIANT WOMEN*
Herron, Don. *THE LITERARY WORLD OF SAN FRANCISCO & ITS ENVIRONS*
Higman, Perry (tr.). *LOVE POEMS*
Hirschman, Jack. *LYRIPOL*
Kerouac, Jack. *BOOK OF DREAMS*
Kerouac, Jack. *SCATTERED POEMS*
Kovic, Ron. *AROUND THE WORLD IN EIGHT DAYS*

LaDuke, Betty. *COMPANERAS*
Lamantia, Philip. *BECOMING VISIBLE*
Lamantia, Philip. *MEADOWLARK WEST*
Lamantia, Philip. *SELECTED POEMS*
Laughlin, James. *THE MASTER OF THOSE WHO KNOW*
Laughlin, James. *SELECTED POEMS*
Lowry, Malcolm. *SELECTED POEMS*
Lucebert & others. *NINE DUTCH POETS*
Ludlow, Fitzhugh. *THE HASHEESH EATER*
Marcelin, Philippe Thoby & Pierre Marcelin. *THE BEAST OF THE HAITIAN HILLS*
McDonough, Kay. *ZELDA*
Moore, Daniel. *BURNT HEART*
Mrabet, Mohammed. *THE LEMON*
Mrabet, Mohammed. *LOVE WITH A FEW HAIRS*
Mrabet, Mohammed. *M'HASHISH*
Murguia, A. & B. Paschke (eds.). *VOLCAN*
O'Hara, Frank. *LUNCH POEMS*
Olson, Charles. *CALL ME ISHMAEL*
Orlovsky, Peter. *CLEAN ASSHOLE POEMS & SMILING VEGETABLE SONGS*
Pasolini, Pier Paolo. *ROMAN POEMS*
Pickard, Tom. *GUTTERSNIPE*
Plymell, Charles. *THE LAST OF THE MOCCASINS*
Poe, Edgar Allan. *THE UNKNOWN POE*
Prevert, Jacques. *PAROLES*
Rigaud, Milo. *SECRETS OF VOODOO*
Rips, Geoffrey. *UNAMERICAN ACTIVITIES*
Rey Rosa, R. *THE BEGGAR'S KNIFE*
Rosemont, Franklin (ed.). *SURREALISM & ITS POPULAR ACCOMPLICES*
Sanders, Ed. *INVESTIGATIVE POETRY*
Shepard, Sam. *FOOL FOR LOVE*
Shepard, Sam. *MOTEL CHRONICLES*
Snyder, Gary. *THE OLD WAYS*
Solomon, Carl. *MISHAPS PERHAPS*
Solomon, Carl. *MORE MISHAPS*
Waldman, Anne. *FAST SPEAKING WOMAN*
Waley, Arthur. *THE NINE SONGS*
Wilson, Colin. *POETRY & MYSTICISM*